Hospitality Management

People Skills and Manners on and off the Job

L Y N   P O N T ,   P H D

Manners Press, LLC

HOSPITALITY MANAGEMENT
PEOPLE SKILLS AND MANNERS ON AND OFF THE JOB

iUniverse books may be ordered through booksellers or by contacting:

iUniverse
1663 Liberty Drive
Bloomington, IN 47403
www.iuniverse.com
1-800-Authors (1-800-288-4677)

Because of the dynamic nature of the Internet, any Web addresses or links contained in this book may have changed since publication and may no longer be valid. The views expressed in this work are solely those of the author and do not necessarily reflect the views of the publisher, and the publisher hereby disclaims any responsibility for them.

Contact information: info@MannersPress.com
www.MannersPress.com
info@MannersForBusiness.com
www.MannersForBusiness.com

Any people depicted in stock imagery provided by Thinkstock are models, and such images are being used for illustrative purposes only.
Certain stock imagery © Thinkstock.

ISBN: 978-1-4917-3308-0 (sc)
ISBN: 978-1-4917-3309-7 (e)

Library of Congress Control Number: 2014910167

Printed in the United States of America.

iUniverse rev. date: 12/29/2014

This book is dedicated to all of you!
You are wonderfully talented and loyal
hospitality management associates.

Thank you for your kindness and dedication.

CONTENTS

AUTHOR'S NOTE

I was speaking to hospitality associates at the Four Seasons Hotel in Miami, Florida, when one very young, very skinny, and very brave associate stood up. He said, "I didn't have a father, so I don't know how to properly button my jacket. Do I leave the last button open? When I need help with things like this, I don't know where to look for answers."

After that tug at my heart, I wrote this career reference book specifically directed at hospitality associates globally. *Hospitality Management: People Skills and Manners On and Off the Job* covers just about every area of the hospitality associate's professional and personal life.

You will learn networking and selling skills; what to expect, wear, and say at funerals; and how to close a conversation, sell your brand, buy a tuxedo, host guests with disabilities, or even come out at work. Condolence and congratulatory letters, where to sit in the corporate jet, petiquette, celebrities, electronic etiquette, life outside of work, and creativity are just some of the topics discussed.

My career background is in human resources management. My master's degree is in personnel administration, and my PhD is in leadership. I am certified in corporate etiquette and international business protocol. As an adjunct professor at two South Florida colleges, I teach business and human resource related topics.

I live in Coral Gables, Florida, on a wonderfully hidden little street where colorful peacocks roam the yard and bright green and blue parrots fly overhead. Through my company, Manners for Business, Inc., I prepare hospitality professionals to represent their brands with polish, politeness, confidence, and authority. My personal mantra for this distinguished industry is to "assume that people will do what's right and always listen with kindness." It would be my great pleasure to hear from you at LynPont@ MannersForBusiness.com.

INTRODUCTION

Creating Amazing Guest Experiences

Hospitality management associates are members of the world's most outstanding team. You are each warm and courteous, and you will create amazing experiences for business and leisure travelers.

You work at hotels, resorts, airlines, restaurants, motels, casinos, bed and breakfasts, country clubs, private clubs, and on cruise ships. You have access to industry training, a career ladder, and equal opportunity. You are a trusted resource. You are exceptional. Now what?

Yours is a very competitive business arena. Being competent is no longer enough. You must stand out—you are representing your well respected brand. Many brands seem comparable, and your guests are looking for cutting edge differences. How will you stand out from the crowd? Simple! Live the rules of both firmly established and creatively innovative business behavior.

My goal is to keep this book simple. I have written it to assist you in promoting yourself and, ultimately, your brand as exceptional. I hope that you will enjoy visiting the basics while concentrating on the special refinements that will delight your guests and have them returning to visit both you and your brand time and time again.

CHAPTER 1

Making a Five Star Impression
The Magical Three Seconds

Jonathan Tisch is the chairman and CEO of Loews Hotels. The man is an icon in defining how to deliver an outstanding overall hospitality experience. In his book *Chocolates on the Pillow Aren't Enough*, he writes, "The link between the hotel and its clientele is one of the most intimate connections between any organization and those it serves" (Tisch 2007).

Wow! Mr. Tisch is telling you that you actually own the power to create a guest experience so wonderful your patrons will want to stay only with you. They will have beautiful memories and elevated expectations, and they will return.

You provide for their bedding, bath accessories, food, shelter, entertainment, technology, koi pond, and more. We know that the towels are fluffy, the bath salts smell great, the food is outstanding, and the fish are delightful. Now it's time to look at just what kind of first impression you want to make that doesn't involve fine linens or exotic bath oils. Psychologists tell us that you have roughly three seconds to make your guests smile. Preparation and planning will lead to success in cultivating a special guest experience.

Your guests will very quickly decide that they know with certainty all about your education, class and social standing, income, race, gender, age, attitude, religion, self worth, place of birth, competence level, and more. Your guests are influenced by your image. Your image is a combination of both your appearance and how you act (Lavington 2001). Your image must say, "There is substance here. You will like me because I am competent, and I can handle any challenge."

The secret to beating those initial three seconds is really simple. Like all the rest of us, your guests enjoy being with people they believe to be similar to themselves and who are on their side. When you are perceived as being the cheering squad of any individual, he or she will be more likely to want to hire you, buy from you, date you, or lend you money (Boothman 2000). All you have to do is create guest confidence. This opportunity begins the moment you step into the lobby!

ENTERING A ROOM

When you enter a room, are you George Clooney or Pee-Wee Herman? Like it or not, you will be watched when you enter a room, any room. You are watched when you enter the lobby to meet your guests. Did you ever notice, at any reception, business or social, that all eyes are on the door? You are representing your brand; people will evaluate you and your brand as you enter the room. You absolutely may not slink off to the bar or to the buffet at a business or social reception.

Excellent posture will create an impression of confidence. Let people know that you are a winner. Remember, those first three seconds count! Never rush into a room. Use your entrance to your advantage. This is an opportunity to be seen as confident and savvy by key persons. This is a business and social opportunity for you as well; you can spot important guests, potential clients, and others with whom you will need to speak during the event.

Your entrance will be powerful if you walk deliberately through the doorway and do the following:

- Once in the room, take one step to the right of the entrance, as there may be others behind you.
- Pause.
- Scan the room slowly, sweeping from right to left and then back from left to right with your eyes.
- Smile. Look pleasant.
- Then take a few steps into the room.
- Briefly think about the several people you have targeted for conversation.
- Smile and head directly toward one of these people (Johnson 2005b).

Yes, you had this planned.

SELF INTRODUCTIONS

Of course you had this planned. Small talk is big business. Prior to any business or social reception, large or small, find out who will be there. Memorize a list of those people you absolutely must meet. So what if it's a social occasion? It's a business opportunity. People are relaxed, and this is the perfect time to say, "Mr. CEO of a Huge Corporation, my name is Five Star Catering Manager of the new Central Park Terribly Trendy Hotel. It's so nice to meet you!"

You must always stand for every introduction unless you are physically unable because you are ill, on crutches, in a wheelchair, or caught in the back of a booth in a restaurant. If that is the case, say, "I'm sorry I am unable to stand." Always use both your first and last names; speak clearly and look directly into your listener's eyes. Smile. Always smile. If Mr. or Ms. CEO is of higher rank and/or is older than you, he/she will extend his/her hand first. Accept the extended hand with a smooth handshake: just two or three pumps from the elbow, not the shoulder.

After introducing yourself, unless invited to do otherwise, address everyone by his or her correct title: Mr., Mrs., Ms., Dr., Father, etc. This is about respect. There is one exception to using proper titles. In North America, if you meet someone who is your counterpart and is approximately your age and rank, you may address this person by his or her first name upon introduction.

INTRODUCING OTHERS

To develop and maintain successful business relationships, know that not all guests appreciate the North American sense of instant familiarity and lack of formality. Rules of formality may be strictly observed in your guest's country. Globally, a proper introduction is a sign that you respect your guest.

Are you able to introduce your general manager and your hotel's best client to one another? Remember to say the name of the most important person first. That would be your client. Any guest or client is the most important person in a conversation with any hospitality associate. The name of your guest is always said first, even when the person being introduced to the guest is the founder of your brand. Clients and guests are always more important than anyone else in your organization.

What about titles? Your guest may be Senator Gibbons or Dr. Meyer. A minister of a Protestant church would be introduced as either Pastor Brown or, if this minister has a doctoral degree, Dr. Brown. Making a mistake about your guest's rank and status would be embarrassing for both of you. As a matter of courtesy, always check the correct form of address before meeting your new guest.

As noted earlier, never address a guest by his or her first name. Your introduction (while looking at Dr. Meyer) would be, "Dr. Meyer, I would like to introduce Mr. Jones. Mr. Jones is the general manager of our hotel." Looking now at Mr. Jones, you would say, "Dr. Meyer visits us from New Orleans several times each year." As the person of superior rank, your guest would extend his or her hand first and say, "Good Morning, Mr. Jones." Mr. Jones would receive the handshake and say, "Good Morning, Dr. Meyer." The North American handshake grip will be moderately firm, and there will be only two or three strokes.

Another proper introduction would be, "Mrs. Evelyn Smith, I would like to introduce Mr. Dane Bernard. Mr. Bernard is the founder and CEO of the Superior Service Hotels." Looking now at Mr. Bernard, you would say, "Mrs. Smith and her family stay with us every Christmas. It's their family tradition."

Seems like a lot to remember to engender respect and ensure your guests' happiness? Happy guests who know they are treasured will return to your property, airline, or cruise line. They will stand by your brand. That's why I recommend that you be prepared. Practice, and you will not only be doing the courteous thing, but you will also present yourself as a relaxed and knowledgeable representative of your brand.

NETWORKING AND MINGLING

Never approach two people who are deep in conversation. It's so much easier to gain rapport with either one person or with a group of three or more. Always ask permission to join the group. "May I join you? My name is Four Star Human Resources Director of the High End Hotel, Toronto. I heard you talking about Cairn terriers. Aren't they wonderful?" Or, "May I join you? My name is Five Diamond Concierge of the Coolest Cutting Edge Hotel, New York, and I've just relocated from London. I'm looking for bungee jumping partners." As you introduce yourself, offer a sincere handshake to each member of the group, complete with a smile and eye contact.

During any conversation, business or social, remember that pauses show you are a thoughtful person and a good listener. Occasional head nodding also shows that you are paying attention. A little frown just once in a while can add weight to your words. When you are assisting guests, you will be smiling most of the time unless this is inappropriate for the situation.

Be prepared to say what you do on property, in just a few attention grabbing seconds. People can lose interest very quickly. You might say, "As a training specialist, I show our associates how to handle themselves flawlessly in guest interactions, because remarkable service is our mission." That particular statement, or a similar statement, is a guaranteed conversation starter.

Don't forget your host, the person who invited you:

- Make yourself known to your host when you arrive at any event, business or social.
- Thank your host for inviting you and shake hands.
- Do not monopolize your host as you enter the event because others need to meet him or her as well.
- When you are about to leave the event, again thank your host for having invited you and for a lovely morning, afternoon, or evening.

A final handshake, a smile, and eye contact are required. This is a sincere but rather quick thank-you, as others will be waiting to speak with your host.

It is important that you always have something interesting to talk about so that your client, guest, or other listener can be made to feel comfortable and informed during his or her stay. After all, that particular person is, at that moment, the center of your world, and you are showering that guest (or potential client) with attention, however short the conversation.

Remember that small talk is big business:

- On property or at a social event, never talk about your health, diet, politics, or religion.
- Do not talk about any controversial subject that might offend your listener or guest.
- Do not ask personal questions or the cost of things.
- Always scan the day's paper, or Internet news headlines and stories, before attending an event or before showing up at work.
- Make sure you are up-to-date on the latest shows, restaurants, art events, and other happenings in town.
- Speak with your concierge. He or she will have creative ideas.

Closing a Conversation

Now you are well into a conversation and realize that your best corporate client is across the room and you must say hello to him or her. You close your conversation with, "I've enjoyed speaking with you, and I hope we meet again." Or, if you have asked permission to telephone the listener during the week with particular information, end with, "I've enjoyed speaking with you and will call you on Tuesday as promised." Again, you will shake hands when closing a conversation, smile, and make eye contact. You've said your good-byes. Simply smile and leave. Do not linger. Now, let's look at your handshake.

THE HANDSHAKE

Are you offering your guests a warm and germ-free welcome? To your guests, you are an expert who projects respect, confidence, and authority. In other words, you are able to attract and maintain guest loyalty with only a handshake.

Why, then, do you insist on coughing into your right hand? This is the hand you will offer to local and international guests, team members, vendors, and heads of state. You will be judged by your handshake while on property and while mingling at a social event.

As you walk across the lobby or pool area—or just make the rounds at an event—your guests and others will see if you are coughing, sneezing, holding a glass of water, scratching, or picking. Why lessen your credibility by reaching for your guest's or potential corporate client's hand and offering him or her either a germ-laden welcome or a wet and cold paper cocktail napkin? Let's keep our right hands not only clean but free of wine glasses, wet paper napkins, purses, briefcases, pens, reading glasses, coffee mugs, and cocktail franks.

Somewhere along the way, a lot of us forgot to carry a basic white linen handkerchief. It is obvious by now that both male and female hospitality associates are watched by their guests. What on earth are you sneezing and coughing into in front of your guests and fellow associates? Run, don't walk, to your local department store and stock up on white cotton or linen handkerchiefs. Buy a bunch! Linen handkerchiefs make terrific and appreciated holiday gifts for your professional friends.

So now that our hands are pristine, what exactly is the perfect handshake?

- The basic handshake worldwide requires you to always stand as a sign of respect.
- Smile, make eye contact, and remember that a great handshake calls for only two or three smooth pumps.
- The web of your hand will touch the web of your guest's hand. Shake from your elbow, not your shoulder.

The person who extends a hand first generally has the power position when introducing himself or herself. In North American business settings, either a man or a woman may initiate the handshake. In social settings in North America and in Europe, a man may wait for a woman to offer her hand. International handshaking is discussed in chapter 14, "Global Etiquette."

How many times have you introduced yourself to someone new only to receive what I call the "Little Princess" handshake? This is when you are offered someone's fingertips. It is obvious this person wants to avoid touching you. Other times it feels as if your new friend is trying to break your hand with the "Hurtful Handshake." Let's not forget what I call the "Preacher's Grip." This is when a perfect stranger shakes hands with you and places his or her other hand on top of your hand. Leave this one for funeral directors and car salesmen; it may seem insincere.

Remember that the person you are being introduced to may have a hidden disability or illness. Be mindful that large rings pressed tightly when shaking hands may cause pain.

LISTENING WITH PASSION

Having your guests and others know that you are delighted that they have shared their needs with you is a huge part of your professional job description. This means you must listen attentively, use the listener's name, maintain comfortable eye contact, and respond pleasantly and appropriately. Before walking away from any conversation with a guest, ask yourself, *Have I listened to my guest without interrupting? Have I asked open ended questions and found or will soon find a solution to the situation? How have I made my guest feel?*

In his book *How to Win Customers and Keep Them for Life,* Michael LeBoeuf, PhD, writes, "Customers will exchange their hard earned money for only two things: good feelings and solutions to problems." In other words, your guest does not want to be sold a three night stay with you (LeBoeuf 2000). On your property, your guest wants to be sold feelings of happiness, comfort, and safety.

In the "Networking and Mingling" section of this chapter, I mentioned the power of the pause. You don't need to talk a lot. Listening with the intent to create a beautiful ending can be the most powerful tool you will ever need to delight a guest.

BUSINESS EYE CONTACT

Great eye contact sends a message of welcome and sincere interest. Lack of eye contact sends the message that you have no time for or interest in the most important person on your property: your guest! When speaking with your guest, you have to ask yourself, *Do my eyes support my words?*

A University of Oklahoma Health Sciences Center study found that in conversation, most people focus on the lower part of the face—the nose, lips, and cheeks. How is this businesslike? Not only is it distracting (for both you and your guest), but exactly what kind of interest in your guest are you communicating by staring at his or her lips? Looking below your guest's eyes sends a strong signal that this is a social interaction.

If this interaction were to take place at a singles function, it would be obvious that you were establishing a degree of intimacy. This kind of interest is further established as your eyes move from your listener's eyes to the chest and down even farther. This type of visual contact is never appropriate in the business arena.

Politely speak with your guest while looking at his or her eyes about 40 to 60 percent of the time. Try looking at an imaginary dot that is placed right between your guest's eyes. This will assist you in professionally controlling the interaction.

Looking at your guest more than 60 percent of the time will make him or her uncomfortable; it will seem as if you are conducting an examination and perhaps being critical. If you look at your guest less than 40 percent of the time, you may appear to be shifty, embarrassed, or shy. It may appear that you are hiding something.

Gracious and professional eye contact tells your guests that you are listening and involved in their stay. The good news is that you will be more positively perceived by your guests and more likeable when you hold your eye contact 40 to 60 percent of the time (American College of Neurology 2000).

PERSONAL SPACE

When approaching your guest to offer your hand, consider personal space. In North America, there are four space oriented zones:

1. *The intimate zone* is a distance of about eighteen inches from one person to another. Save this one for your friends, family, and lovers.
2. *The personal zone* is about one to four feet. Interact with your guests, customers, fellow team members, and friends at this comfortable distance. I call it the cocktail party zone.
3. *The social zone* runs from four to twelve feet. This zone is reserved for strangers, and perhaps the plumber or the UPS delivery person.
4. *The public zone* begins at about twelve feet and extends outward. Use the public zone when you speak in front a group of people (Brown and Johnson 2004).

Each country has its own zone considerations. Global personal space considerations are discussed in chapter 14, "Global Etiquette," as are the basics of international body language, gestures, and handshaking.

Research the customs of your guest's country before his or her arrival to make sure that you present yourself as knowledgeable and respectful.

POSITIVE BODY LANGUAGE

Sparkling body language that communicates authenticity is made of more than good posture and a smile. Dr. Albert Mehrabian, professor emeritus of psychology at UCLA, studied the importance of sending out consistent verbal and nonverbal messages. He found that 55 percent of what your guests will believe and respond positively to takes place visually and involves only your body language.

Your guests are not quite as impressed with your tone of voice. They believe, remember, and respond positively to only 38 percent of what you say based on tone of voice. Your actual words account for only 7 percent of what anyone will remember about what you've said.

Armed with this knowledge, you'll find the rest is easy. Remember that your words, tone of voice, and body language must be in sync for your guests to have confidence in you. These three elements, mixed together, determine how well your listener likes you (Straker 2006).

You can't be tapping your foot impatiently or looking at your watch while smiling and speaking in a soothing voice. Make sure your words, gestures, and tone of voice are all saying the same thing: "I am pleasant and energetic, and I understand what you need. Further, I will see that your stay here is beyond wonderful."

Practice. Observe yourself and others. The first three seconds of any interaction, and handling those three seconds smoothly, are truly the keys to your success both professionally and socially. Stance may send a positive or negative message as well. Keep the following in mind:

- Greet your guest by standing with your shoulders facing his or her shoulders.

- Do not assume a model's pose with one foot in front of the other and your body tilted a little sideways. This is not a shoot for a *Vogue* cover.
- Never place your hands on your hips or cross your arms in front of your body.
- Don't fidget with your fingers or straighten your clothes. A relaxed stance is conveyed when you smile and place your hands by your sides.
- By the way, your mother was right about good posture. It sends out the message that you are confident and prepared.

When interacting with your global guests, there are important multicultural considerations. Worldwide body language, touching, kissing, and international gestures are discussed in the following section on "Gestures" and in chapter 14, "Global Etiquette."

GESTURES

Whatever you do, avoid the okay sign while receiving international guests. The okay sign may signal an unspecified obscenity in Russia, Germany, Brazil, Greece, and Turkey. In France and Belgium, it means that you have no value.

Also avoid the thumbs up sign. This is an offensive and obscene gesture in Australia, Nigeria, Northern Greece, Sardinia, and elsewhere.

Former United States President George H. W. Bush flashed what he thought was the "V for Victory" sign to Australians in 1991. Had he been out and about, he would have been inviting a fight. Don't even nod your head. In North America, a head nod means you are agreeing. On other continents, it can mean that you disagree. Try not to gesture at all.

Unnecessary touching of yourself and others is insulting. Be aware of the following:

- Never pat a child's head. In most countries, only dogs are patted on the head.

- In many countries, there is always the possibility of a sexual harassment or other touching related lawsuit.
- Additionally, ladies, please stop stroking your hair. This takes away from your credibility! Keep your hands at your sides, and for goodness sake, don't touch anyone!

REMEMBERING NAMES

It's useless to say that you aren't good with names. Just slow down and listen intently when a new guest says his or her name. Repeat the name to yourself. See the name spelled out in your mind. Then use this new name in conversation.

An example of using the new name in conversation is: "John Smith is a great name. Of course, you know that Captain John Smith was an important United States historical figure. Are you any relation to that famous family?" Saying the name will help you to remember it.

When you end your conversation with Mr. Smith, be sure to use his name once more. "Mr. Smith, it was a pleasure meeting you and discussing American history." You will not be able to forget Mr. Smith's name. Not only have you repeated it three times, but you have formed an association with the name and you have shown enthusiastic interest in your guest. The next time you see Mr. Smith, you will not have forgotten his name.

Another way to remember a new name is to ask the guest to spell it for you. Sometimes Steven is spelled with a *v* and other times with a *ph*. You'll remember that conversation. Also helpful are memory techniques, such as rhyming or knowing that you have a cousin, a former boyfriend, or a pet ferret by the same name.

Should your guest either not remember your name or not see your name tag, quickly come to his or her aid by offering your hand and a smile while saying your name. Most hospitality associates do not forget their guests' names, or they have a cheat sheet hidden somewhere on their clipboard. Some associates have hidden earpieces and are able to learn their guests' names from another associate who can quietly be reached for immediate assistance.

If you should forget your guest's name, just smile and, while apologizing, ask for your guest's assistance. Allow the guest to graciously save you. In some VIP (Very Important Person) guest situations, a short thank-you note would be in order: "Thank you for graciously coming to my aid this morning, Mr. Jones. I know that you will enjoy your stay with us. Very truly yours, Forgetful Fanny." I'd make sure to leave some very good chocolates with the note.

THE BUSINESS CARD

Business cards are not garage sale flyers. They should be immaculately clean, and all information needs to be up-to-date. Please do not paper a party, private social event, business dinner, or professional meeting with them. You will appear unprofessional and possibly desperate for business. This is not how you want to represent yourself or your brand. Represent yourself and your brand with dignity and class. Your card is an extension of you, and you are an extension of a respected name in hospitality.

Remember the following points when presenting your business card:

- Never give or ask a senior executive for a business card. This person is in a position to request your card if he or she wishes.
- Do not give your card out early in a conversation; you do not yet know your audience. People will generally ask for your card if they are interested in pursuing a business relationship with you.
- Give your business cards to your guests, associates, vendors, and others in a way that they will remember the giver.
- Present the card so that the receiver can read it without having to turn it over or upside down.

And when receiving a business card:

- When you are presented with a business card, look at it carefully; it represents the giver.

- You may want to make a comment about the card—the business location, handsome logo, etc.—before placing it in your own card case, your portfolio, or the breast pocket of your jacket. This is respectful and appropriate conversation.
- Never place a business card in your back pants pocket. In many cultures, this is considered very disrespectful.

Though making notes is an excellent way to remember your new contact, I know that you will not write on the business card in front of the giver.

Carry your cards at all times; business could be lurking anywhere. Your cards need to be in a conservative yet handsome leather card case. I recommend that you place an ample supply of business cards in the pockets of each of your suit jackets just in case you run low at a networking event. I carry business cards in my gym bag; you just never know.

Remember, if the event is a private luncheon or dinner, it would be rude to produce a business card. Be very discreet; you do not want your host to observe you (Johnson 2005b). This is especially true if the event is in a private home. You may wish to offer your card to your new business acquaintance after the private event, as you walk to your transportation.

NAME TAGS

It is traditional for most hospitality management associates to wear name tags. This custom originated in the military as a way to make a soldier's identity and rank readily known. The military name tag is worn high on the left chest area. This seems to work for the armed forces. For the rest of us in the business world, name tags are worn on the upper right chest. This makes sense, as this placement follows the line of sight when shaking hands.

The hospitality management professionals I've asked have no idea why their tags are worn on the left or why guests have to tilt their heads uncomfortably to determine who the associate is. Some brands are gradually shifting this tradition. The whole point is to communicate effectively with your guests. Whichever way your brand has you place your name tag, wear it with pride.

SELLING SOFTLY

Simply by being present, you are selling. The only question is, "What are you selling and how?" Your leisure guests and corporate clients have high expectations. They are looking for value. They are speaking with you because you are either solving a problem they have or providing some service they desire. Engage in conversation. Never simply take an order. You are selling an enjoyable experience with every guest encounter. You are assisting your guests in discovering what's on your brand's menu. This is called *suggestive selling*.

A great example of suggestive selling is when a server suggests to a diner that by ordering a complete dinner, the guest will also receive and enjoy an endive salad made with Roquefort cheese and figs, a chocolate dessert trio, and a lovely bottle of Merlot. Yes, the guest may spend a little more money than if he or she had ordered à la carte. What you are softly selling is the fact that the guest receives more value and a better dining experience by ordering a complete dinner, which you have described in delicious detail (Sanders, Paz, and Wilkinson 2002).

Your guests remember happy occasions. Knowing your guest and your brand's services and amenities enables you to suggest appropriate gifts, babysitting services, outings, and dinners for birthdays, anniversaries, and other celebrations. Your brand may have a computer program that allows you to enter information about your guests, their birthdays and anniversaries, the names of their children and pets, their preferences in vacation spots, tea and wine, and other important facts. Use this cheerful information when greeting your guests. "Mr. Smyth, welcome back. I understand that Rover is joining us again. Please let me know when I may show you and Rover our new Doggie Park." By showing Mr. Smyth the Doggie Park, you are solving what surely would have been a problem for him, and you are adding value to his vacation experience.

Selling softly will connect your guest's happiness with your service and with your brand.

CUSTOMER SERVICE

This section will be really short, because it's not brain surgery. You know this information already because only kind and dedicated people choose a career in hospitality. Your number one job is to make your guests happy. That's it. Making your guests happy will increase revenue for your brand.

The venerable Windsor Court Hotel, an Orient Express property, is situated in wonderful New Orleans, Louisiana. If you didn't know any better, you would think that the historic French Quarter, amazing jazz, remarkable cuisine, Southern charm of the city, and the gorgeous Windsor Court itself are what draw guests to this special property. As I inquired about the various rules hotel associates needed to navigate when responding to guest requests, David Teich, the hotel's general manager, explained, "There are no rules. We do whatever it takes to make our guests happy. It's simple, and it's always the right thing to do."

Happy guests keep returning and sending new guests your way so that your property's occupancy rate soars and every seat in your restaurants, coffee shops, casinos, and airplanes is loyally filled. This is the bottom line; this is why you are in business.

Studies show that most unhappy guests never lodge an official complaint. What they do instead is tell everyone they know horror stories about your brand or organization. Customer dissatisfaction is usually the result of a guest believing that he or she is being ignored (Evenson 2007).

So how do you make your guests happy and create high room occupancy and terrific food, beverage, or full plane revenue for your brand? I'm going to go against conventional wisdom when I tell you to forget about being able to anticipate your guests' needs all of the time. That's just not realistic. Ask your guests what they need. Stop whatever you are doing when you see a guest, and greet him or her by name, with a smile. Ask how you can help to make this stay spectacular. Then listen! You know your business, and you know how to follow up both promptly and thoroughly. Listening with the intent to take action is absolute magic. Please don't forget you also have internal customers, your associates.

It's that easy. I said this would be a short section.

THE POWER OF YOUR WORDS

Simon Cooper is the president of the Ritz-Carlton Hotel Company. He is well known for driving the service excellence and unmistakable quality of Ritz-Carlton hotels worldwide. For him, saying the word *no* is like declaring, "That's not my job." He is passionate when he says, "If it means helping out another or doing something to provide service to the guests, the word *no* is simply not in the vocabulary of those who choose to work at Ritz-Carlton" (Michelli 2008). This is an outstanding statement that reflects the true meaning of superior service, what the Ritz-Carlton organization defines as its gold standard.

The words that you say to your guests and colleagues are very powerful. Think about this: When you were about two years old, your mother began to insist that you use the words *please* and *thank you*. Since that time, nothing has changed except that you now need to use a greater number of nice words. Catch yourself when you begin a sentence with *no*. People generally pay less attention to the rest of any sentence that begins with *no*. Instead, try, "Here's what I can arrange for you right away." So maybe you can't do exactly what your guest requested, but with genuine enthusiasm in your voice and a satisfactory option, the guest will be pleased.

Please remember to use *I* instead of *they* or *we*. Your guest has no idea who *we* and *they* are. He or she sees only you and can't imagine that there are other people hiding behind the reception desk or restaurant podium. Use *I*, and the guest will know that you are responsible for his or her care: "I'm so sorry" and "How may I assist you?" have so much more meaning than "We are so sorry" or "They said it's not the policy."

Another example of the power of your words is the word *spend*, as in: "You would need to spend sixty-five dollars for your son's swimming lessons." Try it this way: "Your investment in Johnny's learning to swim is sixty-five dollars." Well chosen words evoke feelings of guest and colleague trust, appreciation, and loyalty.

Always use the right words in the workplace:

Not So Good	**Better**
"Problem"	"Challenge"
"Could you give me a few minutes?"	"Please allow me a few minutes to arrange that for you."
"I don't know."	"Let me check on that for you."
"I don't know how that could have happened."	"I'm sorry, please allow me to correct this error on your bill."
"I'm sorry."	"Please accept my apologies. I've already corrected your bill."
"I'll do it."	"Right away, Ms. Chen."
"Okay, great, or good idea."	"Excellent choice."
"What?" or "Excuse me?"	"I beg your pardon?"
"Do you understand?"	"I want to be sure that I gave you all of the information."
"May I help you?"	"Please let me know how I may assist you."
"May I put you on hold?"	"Please allow me to place you on a brief hold."
"I'm back."	"Sorry to keep you waiting. How may I assist you?"
"See ya later."	"Have a pleasant morning/afternoon/evening."
"Nite"	"Enjoy your evening."
"Bye-bye"	"Enjoy the aquarium show."
"Hi" or "Hi there"	"Good afternoon."
"Hello"	"Good morning, Ms. Gonzalez, welcome back."

"Hello"	"Hello, Dr. Williams."
"Hello"	"Welcome to the Magic Manor."
"Hello, guys, folks, gals."	"Good morning."
"Hello, you guys."	"Good morning. Isn't this great beach weather?"
"May I take your order, you guys?"	"Good afternoon, it's so nice to see you again. May I tell you about our fresh fish?"
"Are you still working on that?"	"I'll stop by a little later with the dessert menu."
"No problem."	"Of course."
"No problem"	"Please allow me."
"No problem"	"Certainly, my pleasure."
"No problem."	"I would be happy to."
"No problem."	"Absolutely, Mrs. Oliver."
"No problem."	"It would be my pleasure, Mr. Gold."
"No problem."	"Consider it done, sir."
"No problem."	"Certainly, Ms. Wilkins."
"No problem, you guys."	(Don't even think about it.)
Any swear word	(See statement above.)
Gossip	(See both statements above.)

We are not all "guys." You can see that there are no "guys" nor any "problems" in this great industry. Choose your words carefully and watch for results that raise expectations and promote enthusiasm in both your guests and your fellow associates. Remember that few words are well received without two smiles, the one on your face and the one in your voice.

THE UNHAPPY GUEST

Once in a rare while, you will have a guest who is having a really bad day. The thing is, your guests are human. Maybe someone is sick in the guest's family, or your guest has received bad news and seems to be taking it out on you or your property. No amount of special treatment or consideration seems to help. I'm going to go back to my old mantra. Just listen, ask kind questions, and for goodness sake, resolve the challenge quickly and completely.

Please don't put your guest on hold while you sort out the problem. No one wants to feel ignored on top of whatever else is going on in his or her life. If you realize that you are in over your head, excuse yourself and speak with your team leader, supervisor, or whoever else can smooth out the situation.

An important thing about unhappy guests is that they can make you unhappy as well. Never allow yourself to be discouraged. You will probably be able to happily resolve most challenges throughout your hospitality management career. Again, going against conventional wisdom, I am going to tell you the truth. Yes, you will lose a few. Use common sense, kindness, and patience. Unfortunate situations are opportunities to represent your brand with dignity and compassion.

CHAPTER 2

Team Etiquette
A Workplace Culture of Teamwork

Great cultures do not create themselves. As a member of this extraordinary industry, you have graduated from being exclusively a *me*. Now you are also a *we*. You are part of a team driven by a common vision. Now you must think beyond generational, gender, and cultural differences. Instead, think about all that is fine and exceptional in each of your fellow associates. Teamwork is the glue that holds you, your brand, and all of these wonderful people together.

DIVERSITY

Business is gender blind. This means that you have no salesmen, only sales representatives. There are no busboys, only bussers and bus persons. Some establishments no longer use the terms waiter or waitress. The new, state of the art term is *waitron*. You will be safe using the term *server*. No more bellmen either, only bell persons.

You are well mannered and well meaning, so learn the accepted terms for all ethnic and religious groups and nationalities in your workplace. Using slang or sexist terms is the quickest way to offend or hurt your teammates, even if you believe that you are just kidding.

Customs and beliefs vary based on country, region, and religion. These differences can add a richness to the fabric of everyday work life. Being knowledgeable about your associates' differences will not only enrich your own life but will also help you to assist others on your team. If you know that an observant coworker needs to be absent from the property to attend a worship service in the late afternoon, you can schedule your team meeting earlier in the day. If you have an associate who is fasting for religious reasons, you would not invite him or her to a luncheon meeting without first asking if that would be offensive. You might even consider changing the time of your meeting. He or she will be pleasantly surprised and will respect you for being considerate.

There is a tremendous business case for cultivating a diverse team. The hospitality industry reaches a global audience. Isn't it wonderful that your culturally varied associates have just the right soft skills to attract and delight guests from all parts of the earth!

SEXUAL HARASSMENT

Many countries, states, cities, counties, and provinces worldwide have provided guidance regarding the definition of sexual harassment. The United States Equal Employment Opportunity Commission's definition says that unwelcome sexual advances, requests for sexual favors, and other verbal or physical conduct of a sexual nature constitute sexual harassment when submission to or rejection of this conduct explicitly or implicitly affects an individual's employment, unreasonably interferes with an individual's work performance, or creates an intimidating, hostile, or offensive work environment (US Equal Employment Opportunity Commission 1980).

It is each team member's job to cultivate a culture of courtesy and respect. Each individual reading this book is looking out for what is best for his or her exceptional brand. The way to do this is to protect your team, guests, vendors, and any other visitors to your property.

As a supervisor, you have an extra burden. If you even imagine that something is not right, report it immediately to your human resources department. If you are not sure about something you've observed or are afraid you may not have understood a conversation or some office gossip, report it to your human resources department anyway. Be aware that both females and males may be targets of this inappropriate and illegal behavior.

Carefully read your brand's sexual harassment policy. Team leaders, has this policy, and have all policies related to individual dignity, been distributed to and understood by your team? Make sure the team knows how and to whom they must report any concerns of their own. Your brand is not only about excellent guest services, fine food, spacious accommodations, or on time arrivals. It is also about providing a safe and secure work environment for you and your associates.

RELATIONSHIPS AT WORK

Getting along well at work and being liked and respected is not very difficult. The secret is to always be respectful of everyone else. That's it. Well, almost. You also need to be pleasant, helpful, and informed. When you speak with team members, never tell them to do something. Ask them. Say please. Be very polite, smile, and use your coworker's name.

Your coworker may not understand a project that you have explained. Never show impatience. That old saying, "You can catch more flies with honey than with vinegar" is true.

If there is a misunderstanding at work, be truthful about it and have a conversation right away. Never let bad feelings just sit there. The situation only gets worse. Fix it. You have to work with this person every day. Apologize or explain and offer your hand to your coworker. Just be respectful at all times, and people will want to voluntarily assist you since you are always so dependable and kind. Know that everyone has a life separate from the property. Each one of your associates is someone's brother, sister, mother, father, daughter, or son.

DATING COLLEAGUES

As I thought about the subject of dating on the job, I called Maria Ruiz, learning and development manager of the beautiful five star, five diamond, Mandarin Oriental Hotel, in Boston, Massachusetts, and asked her what she thought about it. I first met Maria when she was the senior learning manager of the Four Seasons, Miami, Florida.

After laughing hysterically, she finally said, "That's how I met my husband!" Both she and her intended were working at the Ritz-Carlton, San Juan, as front desk clerks. They fell in love and dutifully reported this development to management. Obviously, she was then carried off into the sunset. I'm going to guess that this is not the usual ending to this story.

Some organizations have the involved parties sign a "Love Contract." This document is between the couple and the company. It states that both parties recognize that workplace romances can have negative effects. The parties agree that the relationship is consensual and promise to do their best to avoid these problems. An office dating policy may require that relationships between associates be reported both to human resources and to each participant's supervisor.

Most organizations do not want supervisors dating their direct reports, and who can blame them? If the romance does not work out, you have all the ingredients for not only a serious conflict of interest but also a sexual harassment lawsuit. Have I mentioned that the entire department's morale can be affected by hints of preferential treatment between coworkers or between an employee and a supervisor?

Here are the rules of the road: Please don't physically touch your love interest at work. No long meaningful glances or giggles during meetings. Check your brand's dating policy. If it requires disclosing the relationship, do so. Think how much better it is for each of you to present yourselves professionally at all times. You are honorable people, and frankly, it is just so much easier to do the right thing than to have to hide behind a potted palm tree should you be spotted together at a bistro some evening.

COMING OUT

The laws protecting the civil rights of gay, lesbian, bisexual, and transgender associates vary widely by country, state, county, and province. You may not be protected from possible termination, a hostile work environment, or an unsympathetic boss or coworker. There is no easy answer except to say that your romantic and personal lives are, and always should be, first and foremost private, no matter your orientation.

If you are wrestling with the decision of coming out or not, find out what your brand's policy is on nondiscrimination. Does it include sexual orientation? Consider the pros and cons before coming out at work.

The pros are great: You no longer have to use gender neutral terms regarding your personal relationships and what you did last weekend and with whom. Since you will no longer have to hide a really important part of yourself, that's one gigantic stress eliminated. Your job performance and confidence levels may actually improve.

The downside, however, is considerable. Think about your nation's culture. Gay rights are not recognized universally, and homosexuality is illegal in several countries. Not everyone is receptive.

Look at your work environment. Is there anyone with authority over you who might not look kindly on your lifestyle? What about your organization in general and your teammates (Belge 2011)? Only you know if coming out to your boss and coworkers is necessary, and only you know if you're ready. There are career counselors who will tell you not to come out at work (Waldman 2005).

My view is simple. People have enough trouble dealing with their own issues. You have integrity and are a proven professional and dependable team member. I have always found hospitality management associates to be a diverse group of warm, caring, and accepting individuals. Assess your need to come out. Also assess your national and work culture and your own comfort level. Will your brand stand by you?

Business is business. Most brands cater to straight, gay, lesbian, bisexual, and transgender guests. You may want to speak with others who have already come out. Think positive. If the water is fine and you want to dive in, you may find that this big dive amounts only to a small splash.

GOSSIP

You are part of a team. Unkind gossip will hurt the effectiveness and closeness of your team. It will erode the trust you have all worked so hard to earn. The best way to avoid having anyone talk about you is to keep personal information personal. If you hear gossip that simply is not true, say so. Let the gossiper know that you are uncomfortable discussing someone else's private life. Criticism of others is a type of gossip and is also unacceptable.

Should you decide to stay and listen to gossip, it makes you a part of the problem. Either change the subject, let the gossiper know you are uncomfortable, or excuse yourself and leave the conversation. I always excuse myself and let the gossiper know that I cannot be associated with this improper discussion. Once you do this, I can promise you that the offender will reconsider repeating this behavior.

CAREER GOALS AND AMBITIONS

To further your personal career goals and ambitions, consider mentoring others with kindness and face work related difficulties with poise. Career success is never earned through envy or by compromising on quality. Earn a spotless reputation by being courteous and excelling in all that you do. Attitude is everything. Everyone remembers the employee who comes through consistently.

Think about what you need, and think about what your brand or property needs. Find a mentor and let this person and appropriate others know your career goals. Learn about your future career pathways by speaking with your human resources representative.

You will be more successful if you develop expertise in one or more areas that are important to your brand. Be flexible. Read, ask questions, attend training seminars. Go back to school if this will position you for a brighter future with the organization. Network within your community and bring in business. Applaud coworker successes.

When the right moment comes, follow your organization's guidelines for applying for a position from within. Let your direct supervisor know what you are doing so that you are supported in your efforts.

Feel genuine joy in your profession—this is the pathway to career success.

SOLICITATIONS AND COLLECTIONS

Your brand probably has a policy regarding office collections, selling your daughter's Girl Scout cookies, or collecting for your favorite charity. Your organization may not allow these kinds of collections. Many companies allow collections only for a charity supported by the brand, such as the United Way.

If collections and sales are allowed, you must conduct these ventures either on your lunch hour or after work and off property. Speak with your team leader in advance. These activities must never interfere with your or anyone else's job duties. Should you not want to contribute to a collection or sales request, say in your most mannerly tone, "Thank you, but not at this time." Smile.

Never distribute any kind of flyer that represents an outside personal interest of yours. That's why your company probably has a "No Solicitation" sign posted outside of the building. Ask your team leader to explain this and any policy about which you are unsure.

EXCHANGING GIFTS

You may want to present a gift to an outside business associate or to one of your team members. Check your company's policy on gift giving and receiving. Very professional gifts include objects that are useful in the workplace (desk calendars, letter openers, paper weights). These are appropriate for outside vendors and associates you wish to recognize for their level of service.

A personal gift is reserved for a coworker who is also a friend, someone you know well. To recognize an associate for a job well done or to remember a birthday or an anniversary, there is no need for a gift. A card signed by the entire department will be appreciated and show the recipient that he or she is respected.

Some departments chip in and purchase a group gift to mark a special milestone. This milestone may be a wedding, the birth of a baby, or a retirement. During the holiday season, some departments conduct gift exchanges. In secret, each team member draws one name and inexpensive holiday gifts are exchanged. Always check both your brand's written and unwritten polices regarding gifts.

CUBICLE ETIQUETTE

All properties and brands dedicate most of their space, and certainly their best space, to guest comfort, business, and entertainment. This means that you may be spending some time working in a cubicle. There is very little privacy in a cube.

Remember that creative cell phone rings, gum popping, pencil tapping, loud conversations, music, perfume spraying, and exotic food odors will annoy your coworkers. Here are the basic guidelines for working in a cubicle:

- Keep social chatting to a minimum and remember that others are listening to your personal telephone calls. Consider making these calls away from your cubicle during lunch or at breaks.
- Avoid the speakerphone when working in a cube.

- When meeting with more than one person, use a conference room out of respect to your fellow cube dwellers.
- Act as if cubicles have invisible doors. Never enter a coworker's cubicle before asking permission to do so.
- Announce yourself and never loiter or appear to be reading someone's computer screen.
- The expression "prairie dogging" means that you peek out above your cube into someone else's cube. Don't even think of doing this.
- If you have a deadline to meet, post a sign at the entrance to your cubicle.
- Use a low voice within your cube, and, of course, never speak to others across cubes.
- Oh, and keep your shoes on! Business etiquette is about respect (Bremer 2004a).

MEETING ETIQUETTE

Meeting etiquette is really easy. Remember those critical initial three seconds? Accomplish the items on the list below and you will show that you respect the person who planned the meeting and that you are organized.

What is most important is that you are there, that you are there on time, and that you are dressed appropriately. Aim to arrive ten minutes before the meeting's starting time. This will give you time to settle in comfortably and introduce yourself to anyone you don't know. Also important as you enter a meeting are the following:

- Never walk into a business meeting with your cell phone or tablet in your hand, talking or checking text messages or e-mails. You will send the message that the meeting is not as important as your telephone conversation, text, or e-mail. You will look unprepared. Never check your smartwatch or other wearable technology during a business meeting.
- Remove your Bluetooth, Google Glass, wireless headset, or other wearable technology before you enter a business

meeting. Take your earbuds out of your ears. Stow your MP3 player, Google Glass, or other visable wearable technology in your briefcase or pocketbook.

- Since you are being watched when you enter a room, why not enter a room smiling, looking confident and approachable?
- Don't go searching for coffee after the meeting has begun; this is disrespectful to the person speaking.
- Review the agenda and be prepared for the meeting by bringing along a pen and notebook, a tablet, laptop, or other electronic devise for note taking.

If this is your first meeting with the group, before you sit down, ask where you are to sit. Sometimes attendees are seated by seniority. Once you are seated at the meeting, keep the following in mind:

- Don't worry about actually taking notes. This is about being ready to participate when the chairperson asks for questions.
- Purses, tote bags, and briefcases should never be placed on a conference table or on a desk. Besides being considered a rude gesture, it makes you look unorganized (especially if you start going through your handbag looking for your lipstick). Place totes/purses/briefcases on the floor during your meeting.
- Remember to keep your elbows off the boardroom table.
- A gentle reminder: no texting, and certainly no iPhone, Android, or other smartphone usage.
- Turn off, or put on vibrate, all electronic devices (other than those used for note taking or presentations).
- If you are expecting an important telephone call, tell the person running the meeting that your cell phone is on vibrate and you may need to briefly leave the meeting. Find a seat close to the door so that you may exit quietly.
- The only time that your smartphone, tablet, electronic notepad, or laptop is ever placed on a conference table is when you are using it to give a presentation, to show your

clients or associates a project related item, or to take notes during the meeting.

- Never use electronics to check your e-mail or surf the Web during a business meeting.
- Never whisper to the person seated beside you; this will appear discourteous to the person who has the floor.
- You may disagree. Never argue. Demonstrate your knowledge, understanding, and professionalism with a short, positive statement about the issue.

At the end of the gathering, thank the chairperson for a productive meeting. Take care of action items resulting from the meeting (Reynolds 2012). Meeting etiquette is not only about respect but also about efficiency in getting the agenda's goals accomplished. The meeting will fly by without electronic interruptions.

Your organization may send out computerized calendars that advise you when meetings will be held. The calendars may also allow you to respond to the meeting invitation. Other organizations are not that structured, and you may be invited at the last minute. Try to attend. If you are truly unable to attend, you might want to request a copy of the minutes or a report of the meeting (Post 2004).

LEADING A TEAM MEETING

Start your meeting on time. You are showing respect for the attendees, and you are showing that you are a professional. It may be that your organization's style has been a little last minute. Try setting the tone for your own meetings by sending out meeting invitations along with an agenda well in advance of your meeting date.

Think carefully about setting the day and time of your meeting. Mornings are tough; everyone is so busy. I am not a fan of Fridays when everyone seems pressed for time. Some experts believe that meetings work best in the afternoon (Post 2004). Just give everyone as much notice as possible, and distribute agendas in advance. The most important thing is to stick to your agenda. That way, you'll stay on time and on track.

CHAPTER 3

Celebrations
Sharing the Joy

At times throughout your hospitality career, you will receive invitations to attend your coworkers' and your friends' happy life changing events. This may or may not mean that you must attend these joyful events or that you must provide an endless stream of presents. This section was created to guide you along the road of some very traditional celebrations set in today's sometimes nontraditional world.

WEDDINGS

A wedding can be the happiest day in the lives of the bride and groom. Weddings may be elaborate or understated, formal or casual. Weddings come in all shapes, and one size does not fit all. The ceremony can be religious, military, or civil, or it may be a commitment ceremony between two women or two men.

Before the wedding, an engagement party may be hosted by the bride's parents. While the couple's friends may give an engagement gift if they wish, it is not expected. Engagement presents are given only by the couple's closest friends and family members. Engagement gifts are sent to the home of the bride; they are not brought to the engagement party.

You may also be invited to a bridal shower given by the bride's friends. Friends who are invited to bridal showers bring a present to the party. Since buying both a shower gift and a wedding present can be financially difficult, see if you and others on the team can go in together to purchase one lovely wedding gift.

At all of these parties, your job as a guest is to be supportive, be on time, and enjoy a wonderful experience.

Gifts

Wedding presents are sent before the wedding. There is a myth that you have up to a year to send a wedding gift. This is incorrect.

Never bring a gift with you to a wedding. It is considered a breach of etiquette. The happy couple is too busy glowing to accept, open, store, and/or mail gifts back home. Gifts are brought only to bridal and baby showers and children's birthday parties. Have the store send the gift to the bride's home, or go to the post office yourself with the gift.

Gifts are addressed to the bride and sent to her in care of whomever issued the invitation. It is just not possible to put her address on the wedding invitation in addition to all that is already on there. If your gift is obtained through a bridal registry, then you know you have the preferred mailing address.

If a group from the property is attending, then it is not only proper but good common sense to chip in for one nice gift. You do not have to send a gift if you are not attending the wedding. A congratulatory card with a handwritten note inside is proper. If you are a family member or close friend, it is appropriate to send a gift even if you are unable to attend the ceremony.

Money as a Gift

There are some ethnic groups for whom gifts of money are appropriate as a wedding gift. If presented prior to the wedding, the check is made out to the bride. If the check is taken to the wedding, it is presented to either the bride or groom while in the receiving line, and it is made out to either the bride, the groom, or both.

The Wedding Announcement

While close friends and family often respond with a present, presents are not required when you receive an engagement or wedding (or birth of a baby) announcement. Nor are presents required if you decline attendance at a wedding (or other event). You need send a gift only if you actually attend the wedding or if you are fond of the bride and/or groom and unable to attend the nuptials.

The Invitation

Answer the wedding invitation within one week of receipt. The invitation may advise, on the lower right hand corner, that the party is "black tie" or "black tie optional." The meaning of these terms will be discussed in chapter 11, "The Power of Your Wardrobe," in which we will talk about what you, the savvy professional, will wear for both work and social occasions.

The Rehearsal Dinner

Generally, only out of town guests, the bridal party, local family members, and the closest of friends are invited to the rehearsal dinner. It is customary for this reception to be given by the groom's family. Depending on both the financial and geographical circumstances, the bride's family may host this dinner. If the couple being married is older or more established, they may host both this party and the wedding itself. The upcoming wedding ceremony is practiced by the bridal party, and then the guests have a dinner, complete with traditional toasting to the couple.

The Ceremony

The ceremony may take place in a church, rectory, synagogue, mosque, meeting hall, hotel, country club, judge's chambers, private home, military chapel, or on a beach. Arrive at least fifteen minutes early for the ceremony. If there is a guest book, the guest signs his or her name without a title (no Mr., Mrs., Ms., Miss, or Dr.). Sign it "Lyn and Edwin Carter." You may also leave a little message just to the side of your name, such as "Much happiness" or something similar and very short.

For an indoor wedding, there may be ushers at the door who will walk you to your seat. You may be asked if you are a friend of the bride or a friend of the groom. This question is generally asked at formal weddings. Friends of the bride are traditionally seated on the right side of the church, synagogue, or hall, and friends of the groom are seated on the left.

Usually the groomsmen, best man, and groom (sometimes escorted by his parents) enter first. Then the bridesmaids, maid of honor, and matron of honor enter the sanctuary. The bride, usually escorted by either her father or both parents, enters last. This happy trail of people can be large or very small. This entering group is called the *processional*. In many religions and cultures, the congregation stands when the processional begins. Be aware, though, that in some faiths you do not stand when the processional begins. If you are unsure, watch the couple's family members (usually seated in the first two rows) for guidance.

When the ceremony is complete, the happy couple, immediately followed by the entire bridal party, exit the room. This is called the *recessional*. Allow the guests seated in the first rows to exit first, with subsequent rows following. There may be a receiving line immediately after the ceremony.

The Receiving Line

The purpose of the receiving line is to give the bride and groom an opportunity to formally greet every person who attended their wedding ceremony. It's generally made up of the bride's and groom's parents, then the bride and groom, followed by members of the bridal party. Sometimes the receiving line is much shorter.

Walk through the receiving line. Do not take a drink with you. Introduce yourself to the family. Say something like, "The ceremony was just beautiful." Never congratulate the bride. Wish the bride "much happiness." Offer your congratulations to the groom.

At large and very formal weddings, the guests may first be directed to stand in a smaller line called a *reception line.* The reception line leads to the receiving line. In the reception line, an introducer will ask your name and walk you over to the receiving line. He or she will whisper your name to the first person in the receiving line; this is usually the bride's mother. The bride's mother then introduces you to the next person in line and so on.

Table Number Cards and Place Cards

At large weddings and other events, table number cards are placed into small envelopes, which are arranged in alphabetical order on an entry table. The guest takes the envelope that has his or her name written on it. Inside the envelope there is a card on which the table number is written. These envelopes and their contents are sometimes referred to as *escort cards.*

A place card is about the size of a business card. Each guest's name is written on an individual place card, which may be preset on the dining tables. Never trade places with another guest if you have been assigned a specific place at the table.

At formal weddings (and other formal dinners), only the guest's last name and title is used: Ms. Gardener, Dr. Suarez, Mayor Silver. At informal weddings and dinners, the guest's first and last names are used: Susan Gardener, George Suarez, Jonathan Silver.

Dancing

No matter what, the first dance belongs to the bride and groom. Then, traditionally, the bride dances with her father and the groom with his mother. Depending on the formality of the wedding, eventually fathers, daughters, mothers, fathers, and in-laws all dance with each other. After the bridesmaids and ushers have started to dance, all guests may enjoy the dance floor.

Toasting

The toasting begins with the dessert course at a formal lunch or dinner reception. For an afternoon reception, the toasting begins when the couple has had their first dance. The best man is the toastmaster, and he has prearranged the number of people toasting. He makes the first toast. Then the groom toasts the bride and the bride toasts the groom. The bride's father is next.

Toasts should be short. They may be sentimental or they may be witty, but they are never suggestive or embarrassing.

Cutting the Cake

The polite guest never leaves a wedding until the cake is cut. The cake is cut right before the dessert course is served. Or the cake may be the lone dessert.

At an afternoon reception, the cake is cut after the toasts have been made. The bride and groom take turns feeding each other a little bit of the cake and then slices of cake are cut and served to the guests.

Suggestion: See that the couple is supplied with a fork to use when feeding each other cake. No bride wants to look at her wedding pictures and see icing on her face, fingers, and possibly her gown.

Throwing the Bride's Bouquet

Traditionally, the bride throws her bouquet to her attendants and other single female guests at the end of the wedding. Custom has it that the woman who catches the bouquet will be the next to marry. At some weddings, the groom removes the bride's garter from her leg and throws it to his ushers and other single male guests. The thought is that this man will be the next to marry. Since some brides are uncomfortable with this activity, it is up to the bride and groom to decide if they wish to include taking the garter off the bride's leg as a part of the reception. Should anyone ask, I did not include this less than elegant act as a part of my own wedding celebration.

Your Job as a Guest

Unless you have been specifically asked to do so, please do not take pictures during the wedding ceremony. This is an etiquette blunder and is actually very annoying to the rest of us. Taking pictures during the ceremony is the job of the official wedding photographer.

The bride and groom may have hired a professional videographer. With this in mind, if your children have specifically been invited to the wedding (their names are on the invitation), please consider whether they are old enough not to interrupt the ceremony. Do you really want your dear friends to hear a crying child on their wedding soundtrack?

Remember to find and thank the hosts of the wedding before you leave the party. I know that you will handwrite the hosts a thank-you note (right away) letting them know how lovely the wedding was and how much you enjoyed it.

MATERNITY

Maternity is such a blissful time. If you are the expectant mom, you will want to shout loudly about your happiness. Just don't do this at work. You'll need to tell your team leader or supervisor about your happy condition as soon as reasonably possible. You will have to plan your upcoming leave.

In the United States, if you have been employed for more than one year and your location has more than fifty employees, you may be covered by the federal Family Medical Leave Act (FMLA). You may still qualify if your site has fewer than fifty associates as long as your brand has other locations within seventy-five miles of where you work. In this case, these additional employees are counted (along with you) as part of the required fifty associates.

FMLA allows men and women up to twelve weeks of unpaid leave after the birth or adoption of a child. Discuss leave eligibility and details with a human resources department representative, as you may or may not be covered by FMLA.

Note to new moms and dads: Please don't show us a never ending parade of pictures. We already know the kid is cute. Remember that too many baby stories will cause our eyes to glaze over. Your friends will want to see the baby, but please, don't bring your new baby to your property or office unless your department head has given prior approval. If so, make it a short visit that does not overly interrupt the workday.

It is appropriate for the entire team to purchase a small gift for the new arrival and for all to sign a congratulatory card. If the hospital stay will be short, send the card to the home. Otherwise, send the card to the hospital. Have the store deliver the gift to your colleague's home so that she will not need to hire a moving company to ferry herself, the new baby, and the mound of gifts, boxes, flowers, and cards she will be accumulating. Factor in the staff's individual financial constraints when choosing a suitable gift to which the team contributes.

Should the pregnancy end in a miscarriage or a loss of the baby at birth, those associates who are personally close to this team member may individually wish to take their friend out for lunch or dinner upon her return. It would be appropriate to say, "You were missed at work, and I'm so glad that you are feeling better." Or, "I am so glad that you're back. I'd like to take you to lunch on Friday." Never ask questions. Do not overwhelm your friend with sadness upon her return. The same kindnesses are extended to male associates returning to work after this loss.

If your friend is home recovering from this loss, a short handwritten note is always appropriate. Please do not send an e-mail, as she may assume that you require a response and she may not be up to this. A brief note will do:

> *Dear Susie:*
> *I am thinking about you and look forward to your*
> *return. When you are caught up with work, you and*
> *I will have dinner.*
> *Warm wishes,*
> *Franklin Friend*

BABY SHOWERS

You and other department members will probably want to throw your joyful teammate a baby shower. Baby showers are best held away from work, after business hours. Arrangements should be made quietly so as not to interfere with work. The other option is a cake, a card signed by everybody, and one present from everyone given to the expectant colleague either during lunch or at a convenient time agreed to by your department head.

Remember that it is the thought that counts. Your group gift does not have to cost lots of money. It does have to be well thought out and meaningful. Gifts of either a baby book or a silver picture frame are lovely to receive. It is not necessary to give both a shower gift and a baby gift. Generally that combination of gifts is given only by close friends and family.

BAPTISMS AND CHRISTENINGS

A baptism ceremony welcomes the baby into Christian life. A christening is a baptism in which the baby is named. The baby will be presented in a white christening gown that may have been handed down from generation to generation. In Catholic churches, the baptism is generally a specially arranged ceremony. For Protestants, baptisms are held during regular church services. Older children and adults may be baptized as well.

You may be invited to a christening party. These receptions may be small and held in the home of the family. You may be served punch or Champagne. There is usually a beautifully decorated christening cake. Sometimes very large and elaborate receptions are held.

Often the christening is held within a month or so of the baby's birth, so an additional gift is not expected. Customary gifts are typically religious in nature—a Bible or religious figurine or other religious baby jewelry. If your gift was not sent to the parents' home earlier, leave it in your car during the ceremony. Bring it with you to the christening party.

JEWISH NEWBORN CEREMONIES

Brit Milah/Bris

Jewish male babies are circumcised on the eighth day after birth. This circumcision is called a *Brit Milah* or a *bris*. The words in Hebrew means "a covenant of the son." A covenant with God is made to rear the child in the Jewish faith.

The bris can be performed in a synagogue, private home, catering hall, hotel, or hospital. This is a religious occasion where men are asked to wear a head covering called a *yarmulke*. The yarmulke is worn as a sign of respect for God. All male attendees will be given a yarmulke to wear.

Guests are generally invited by telephone, since the timing between the ceremony and the birth itself is so close. Today, with so many births being planned, some parents are having invitations made up ahead of time. They send out the invitations the moment the baby is born.

There will be a joyous celebration following the bris and again, like a christening, the type of celebration can range from a small reception to a very elaborate event. Gifts for the newborn baby boy are either sent to the parents' home or brought to the bris itself.

Brit Bat/Naming Ceremony

Female Jewish babies have a naming ceremony that takes place within the first month of life. The child receives her name, and a covenant with God is made to rear her in the Jewish faith. The naming ceremony is called a *brit bat*, meaning "covenant of the daughter."

The parents or grandparents generally host a reception. Like a bris and a christening, the reception can be small, or large and elaborate. Gifts for the baby are appropriate and are either sent to the parents' home or are brought to the naming ceremony itself. If you have just given the family a baby gift at the child's birth, then a second gift is not necessary.

ISLAMIC NEWBORN CEREMONY

Muslims may hold a birth ceremony (an *akikah*) to welcome the newborn. Men and women guests will almost always sit apart from one another. It is important to dress very conservatively if you are invited to this happy occasion. It is respectful for a woman to wear a scarf to cover her head, and dress hemlines must be below the knee. Women who are not Muslim might not be asked to cover their heads. The event may be held at the mosque or in the home of the parents or grandparents. Bring your baby gift with you to the akikah (Post 2004).

CATHOLIC FIRST COMMUNION

At the age of seven, a Catholic child receives his or her First Communion at a regular Sunday morning service called a *Mass*. The child is given what is called the *Sacrament*. This is bread and wine that represents Christ's body and blood and unites the child with Christ.

Generally, family members and close friends are invited to the child's First Communion. Gifts are appropriate; books, games, and religious items are appreciated. Leave your gift in the car, and after the Mass, bring it with you to the breakfast or brunch that usually follows in a nearby restaurant. The meal is generally given by the parents, but the grandparents or godparents may do this as well.

BAR OR BAT MITZVAH

After considerable study, and generally at the age of thirteen, Jewish boys and girls celebrate either a *bar* or *bat mitzvah* ("son or daughter of commandment"). After much rehearsal, a ceremony that can last from one to three hours is held at a synagogue. The teen reads to the congregation from the Old Testament in Hebrew. He or she also prepares and reads a speech about accepting the responsibilities of Jewish adulthood. The ceremony generally takes place on a Friday evening or on a Saturday. This event is considered of utmost importance to the family.

The service is followed by a reception of some kind. Often, all service attendees are invited to a meal right after the service. This reception is held in the synagogue hall. Other families additionally give a luncheon or dinner in a hotel, restaurant, or banquet hall.

These can be very formal affairs with a band or disc jockey and elaborate decorations and flowers.

Your gift will be very much like a birthday gift. Today, children receive books, money, articles of clothing, cell phones, tablets, and even computers.

PROTESTANT AND CATHOLIC CONFIRMATION

Christian children formally become members of their congregation when they are confirmed, generally at the age of twelve or thirteen. Catholic children study hard for this most important day when they will be quizzed about their faith. Usually only family and the very closest of friends are invited to the confirmation. Those invited to the ceremony present gifts (books, appropriate religious objects, and items of clothing). It is traditional for Catholic godparents to host a lunch afterward.

Most Protestant churches conduct confirmations during regular church services. The child confirms the vows of membership that were said for him or her as an infant. He or she is then formally recognized as an adult member of the church. Again, only family and the closest of friends present gifts. Confirmations are very happy occasions.

JEWISH CONFIRMATION

Jewish teenagers are confirmed at the age of sixteen or seventeen. After a period of study, Jewish teenagers are able to understand and practice the religious principles of their faith. The ceremony itself is held at the synagogue; it may be held as part of the regular Saturday morning or Friday night services or as a separate event. It is not an individual ceremony. It is conducted for the entire confirmation class.

Usually only family and the very closest of friends are invited. Only family and those friends invited to the ceremony present gifts (books, appropriate religious objects, and items of clothing). In the

United States, many confirmation classes take a fun, chaperoned, two or three day senior trip together. The trip may be to a theme park like Walt Disney World.

BIRTHDAYS

In the office, you probably already have an established way of celebrating birthdays. Usually a cake and a card signed by the group are presented to one of your team members on his or her birthday. For very large departments, all birthdays falling in the same month may be celebrated with one cake on the same day. Gifts will not be expected. Have a wonderful celebration, and be sure that you time the event to coincide with a break or meal period. Always prearrange the timing with your department head.

If you attend a children's birthday party, bring the gift with you to the party. Make sure that the gift is appropriate to the child's age.

SWEET SIXTEEN

This party is held for girls when they turn sixteen years of age and is generally hosted by the girl's parents. The celebration can be only for girls or it can be coed. Parties are held in homes or at movie theaters, restaurants, hotels, pizza parlors, skating rinks, and swimming pools. The party may be an all girls luncheon or an elaborate, formal occasion for both boys and girls, complete with a live band.

If you are an adult and are invited to a sweet sixteen party, you are either a family member or a very close friend. Expect to serve as a chaperone. Bring a birthday gift of clothes, jewelry (real or costume), or a gift certificate with you to the party.

DEBUTANTES

Today's debutantes celebrate finishing their first year of college or last year of high school as a group. The word *debutante* is derived from the word *début*, "to come out." In days past, being presented at a debutante ball meant that the girl was now ready to find a suitor.

Today, the ball is a presentation into society and has nothing to do with getting married.

In the past, it was common for each debutante to have her own formal ball. Today, parents of debutantes generally belong to a charity that will sponsor the party for these young women as a group. The parents donate a certain amount of money, and invited guests purchase tickets. The events are excellent fundraisers.

The girls practice dancing and social etiquette to prepare themselves not only for the ball but for a successful social life as well. The balls are elaborate and formal affairs. Each debutante will have one or more escorts. There may also be ushers, flower girls, and pages in attendance.

Everyone has a wonderful time at a debutante ball. If you are invited to this lovely occasion, you are either a close friend or a relative. Give a nice gift of costume (or real) jewelry or articles of clothing (Baldrige 2003). Send your gift to the debutante's home.

QUINCEAÑERA

The *quinceañera* (also called a *quince*) represents the fifteenth birthday of a Hispanic or Latina girl. This is a very big deal. There may be a religious ceremony prior to the party. The party itself can be a very elaborate, formal occasion that calls for an orchestra and for guests to wear tuxedos and formal gowns.

This event is so important that no matter the income level of the family, the girl is dressed beautifully, and a party of some kind is held. Young girls look forward to this magical day and plan their party for years in advance of the actual event.

Send your present to the girl's home. This present is equivalent to what you would give for a sweet sixteen party, although it is also traditional to give money. Go and enjoy yourself at this spectacular celebration.

THE HOLIDAY PARTY

It's that time again—you've been invited to attend your property's or organization's holiday bash, or perhaps to the home of your general manager to toast the New Year. I've established some exacting guidelines so that your fine and well earned reputation remains just that way.

There are only six important things to remember:

1. You must attend.
2. You must stay sober.
3. Dress appropriately.
4. Mingle.
5. Prepare your spouse, significant other, date, or partner for whatever is to come.
6. Handwrite a thank-you note to the appropriate person (Pachter 2008).

No, you may not e-mail or text a thank-you note. You are special, not ordinary. Go and have a wonderful time at the party. The advice in this section of course applies to all business and social occasions, including office parties, to which you are invited throughout the year.

GRADUATION

When you receive either a high school or a college graduation announcement, your only obligation is to respond with either a card or letter of congratulations. If you receive an invitation to the graduation itself, it is customary to send a gift to the graduate. Graduation parties are usually given by the parents for the graduate and his or her friends.

If a colleague at work graduates from college, recognizing this accomplishment at a staff meeting or private departmental gathering would be the right thing to do.

WORK RELATED ANNIVERSARIES AND RETIREMENT

Your brand may celebrate work related anniversaries of five years and greater. These may be small departmental affairs celebrated by giving the recipient a five year pin or other acknowledgment. If you are the manager and your employee is celebrating even a one year anniversary, an announcement at your morning meeting is sure to bring smiles to everyone.

Often the event is recognized in newsletters, on company intranet sites (these are in-house Websites), at employee pep rallies, and at quarterly and other important gatherings where individual associates are acknowledged and congratulated for their longevity with your brand. Your colleague will receive very public best wishes. Individual gifts are not expected, but a heartfelt "congratulations" will be appreciated by your associate. Celebrations of an anticipated and well deserved retirement are also recognized in this way. Find out what your brand's traditions are.

YOUR FAMILY'S AND FRIEND'S PERSONAL MILESTONES

So far, most of what you have read is directed to your life at work. Yet you could never be successful at work if you did not have terrific people in your life way before you started with your brand. In your personal life, remember important dates in the lives of those who are close to you. Don't forget anyone. Keep everyone's important dates on a calendar, personal digital assistant, or cell phone. An anniversary card or handwritten note is a wonderful acknowledgment for family and friends. Remember to send family members and friends a note or a card for a promotion, retirement, or winning soccer team. Of course, a follow-up congratulatory telephone call will be well received.

CHAPTER 4

Rites of Passage
Life's Challenges—Personal and Professional

There will be emotional, intellectual, personal, spiritual, and work related changes throughout your career. This section will assist you in appropriately participating in the unfortunate challenges that continue to make up your own personal and professional rites of passage.

HOSPITAL ETIQUETTE

At some point in your career, one of your associates (or a friend or family member) may be hospitalized. Most of us are uncomfortable around illness. However, as a representative of your property or brand, you may be asked to visit your ill coworker at the hospital. It's your job to be pleasant and smile while visiting. The following are some of the basics when you visit someone in the hospital:

- Remember not to wear perfume or cologne, and don't even consider visiting if you are sick or even imagine that you are coming down with a cold.

- Call the nurse's station and inquire before bringing food, even if the patient has requested the food. He or she may be on a restricted diet.
- Ask the nurse if bringing flowers or a plant is permitted. Your associate or his or her roommate (if it is not a private room) may have allergies.
- If you do bring flowers, bring along a vase. I don't know where your bedridden colleague, friend, or family member is supposed to find a vase for cut flowers.

I probably don't need to tell you not to eat any of the food that you have brought as a gift, but certainly never eat from a hospital food tray and don't nibble on food others have brought. Besides the etiquette of the thing, maybe there should be a sanitation concern on your part.

When you arrive, do not sit on the bed, and if there are not enough chairs, just stand. This is going to be a short visit anyway. Take your coworker's or friend's hand (after asking if you may) in a warm and very gentle greeting. No hugs! Your associate is sick. Out of consideration to other patients, speak audibly but also softly. In these close quarters, anyone in the hall may be able to hear your private conversation.

Of course, if a physician, nurse, or other health care professional needs to attend to the patient, excuse yourself from the room. Many hospitals do not allow cell phone use. Please respect this regulation, or you may be asked to leave.

Should your ill associate want you to take him or her for a walk or a spin in the wheelchair, go to the nurse's station and make sure that this is permitted. No matter how important your question is, the staff may be overworked. Sound familiar? The nurse may not be able to get back to you right away. Politely ask again a little later.

Think about the gift that you take with you. Don't bring a book or magazines, for example, if your friend has just had eye surgery (SIGA 2013). Never bring children on your visit. Consider how ill the patient is before bringing your teenage child with you. If your teen is accompanying you, brief him or her on appropriate hospital behavior. Even with all good intentions, limit the number of guests visiting to no more than two at a time.

People always wonder, "How long shall I visit and what do I say?" Consider the following:

- Try not to stay over ten minutes. If your coworker is well on the way to recovery, you may stretch the visit by a few minutes. There are times when five minutes is appropriate.
- If relatives are there, you may want to stay for a shorter time to allow the family to be together.
- Keep your conversation as upbeat as possible, and remember that no one wants to hear about your earlobe, foot, or gall bladder surgery.

FUNERAL ETIQUETTE

It is unfortunate, but at some point in your career, you may lose a member of your team or someone close to your team. You may lose a friend or a family member. You may be called upon to represent your property, brand, or family at a funeral. This is a difficult time, and it is important to be comfortable in knowing how to conduct yourself.

Funeral traditions of some of the world's major religions are reviewed in this chapter. If you are not familiar with the religious customs of your departed friend or colleague, research these before attending the funeral service.

Wakes

Some religions have wakes, or viewings, a day or two prior to the funeral. Sign the reception book as you enter the funeral home so that the family knows you were there. It is up to you whether you wish to view the body, as wakes often have open caskets.

The family members will be seated in one area. Introduce yourself to the family. They are waiting to receive you and other mourners. State your relationship to the deceased. Say something appropriate like, "I am so sorry. John was very special to all of us at the hotel." Or, "My prayers are with you." Then move on, as others must also pay their respects to the family. Never say, "My goodness, what happened?" Never ask, "How did he die?" or "Was he ill for a long time?" Your job at this occasion is to provide comfort.

Cremation

Certain religious groups do not conduct cremations. For those that do, there is generally a church service prior to the cremation. After the funeral service, just the family and the closest of friends attend a short service at the crematorium.

The family generally receives visitors at home following the cremation. The hours of visitation at the family's home are announced by the funeral director at the end of the church service.

The Burial

Funerals may be held at a church, synagogue, mosque, or funeral home. The burial at a cemetery follows immediately, and it is considered good manners to attend the burial in addition to the funeral service. If you are attending the burial, get into your car right after the funeral service and follow the funeral procession to the cemetery. There is always a police escort for the funeral procession. Cars in the procession will be asked to turn on their headlights. Some families keep it simple by having the entire service at the graveside.

Sending Flowers

You and your colleagues may decide to send flowers. It is traditional to send a wreath to the funeral home. Another option is to send a conservative arrangement to the family of the deceased. Sending flowers is not a part of either Jewish or Muslim tradition. Often families will suggest sending a donation to a charity in lieu of flowers.

Jewish Traditions

Jewish families sit shiva anywhere from two to seven days. *Shiva* means "seven" and represents the time that traditional Jewish people welcome mourners into their homes. There will be a pitcher of water either at the cemetery or outside of the home. Before leaving the cemetery, or when you arrive at the home after a Jewish funeral, rinse your hands from the pitcher. This is a symbolic cleansing.

The mirrors in the home may be covered. This represents keeping your thoughts on the deceased and not on vanity. Orthodox Jews have little wooden stools you may sit on as a sign that you are not thinking of your own comfort. Mourners may also wear socks but not shoes in the house of the deceased. Again, it is about quiet observance, not comfort.

It is traditional to send food and baked goods, as the mourners are in grief and should not be cooking for their guests. Sending flowers is not a part of the Jewish tradition. A donation to an appropriate charity will be appreciated.

Catholic Traditions

If your coworker was Catholic, go to the family's church and purchase a Mass card in his or her name. The church will then celebrate a Mass in your friend's name. A Mass is the central act of worship in many Christian churches. During a Mass, bread and wine are blessed and consumed in remembrance of Christ's death. Send the Mass card to the family. They will find comfort in your kindness when they attend this special Mass that you and your team have arranged. Mass cards provide all of the information the family needs regarding the day, date, and time of this ceremony.

The pallbearer is a person who helps carry the casket at a funeral. Should you be asked to be a pallbearer at the funeral, you must accept, as this is a great honor. Your participation is also a way of honoring your deceased friend, family member, or colleague. Catholic families receive visitors in their homes after the funeral.

Protestant Traditions

Protestant families receive mourners in their homes after the funeral. As with a Catholic funeral, it is a great honor to be asked to act as a pallbearer.

Muslim Traditions

If your coworker was Muslim, the funeral service will be held within twenty-four hours of his or her passing. Muslims are not cremated. The service is open to all mourners and is conducted after the funeral procession and the noonday prayer.

Men and women may be asked to sit apart from one another. It is respectful for women to wear a scarf to cover their heads, and dress hemlines must hit below the knee. Women who are not Muslim may not be asked to cover their heads.

Attend this service and offer your condolences to the family. The funeral procession itself may be all male and is conducted on foot, not by car (Ingram 2005). Sending flowers is not a part of the Muslim tradition. A donation to an appropriate charity will be appreciated.

Memorial Services

Memorial services are held after the deceased has already been interred. The funeral may have been private, or it may have been held in another town. The memorial service gives those who were not at the funeral or cremation a chance to honor the deceased and to pay their respects to the family.

There is generally a clergyman leading the memorial service. Two or more individuals are asked to speak briefly about the deceased. Being asked to speak is a special honor. If the family will be receiving guests in their home or another location after the service, this will be announced prior to the end of the memorial service.

If You Are Asked to Speak

If you are asked to speak, whether at a funeral or a memorial service, you may not be given much advanced notice. Keep your remarks short, three to five minutes. Your remarks must be comforting and respectful. Consider telling a story that will make the family smile as they remember the departed's special love for animals, tennis, or volunteer work. Should you become emotional and unable to continue, simply say "I'm sorry" and step down from the podium.

Visiting the Family

When the funeral service ends, a representative of the funeral home will announce when and whether the family will be receiving visitors. Visitors are usually received at the family's home, but they may also be received at a social or catering hall, hotel, or other location. Whatever the religion, research the traditions before attending the funeral or visiting the family.

How to Dress

This is a solemn occasion, so dress conservatively for a funeral or a wake. Dark colors are a sign of mourning and of respect. Women should wear suits, long pants, pantsuits, knee length dresses, or knee length skirts. It is not appropriate to show a lot of skin. Men should wear a dark suit or a jacket and tie.

SEPARATION AND DIVORCE

Divorce or separation can happen to anyone, so know that your colleague is experiencing a spectrum of feelings: sadness, fear, loss, loneliness, failure, uncertainty, or even relief. Never say, "What happened? You and Thomas seemed so happy." Instead say, "I'm so sorry. Is there anything here at work that I can do for you?" Then follow through. Do not ask personal questions. If the person becoming divorced is a close friend, then of course you two will discuss the divorce, but not at work.

If you are the person going through a separation or divorce, never discuss personal details at work. Let your supervisor know about your situation. This is important, as you may need time off to handle related matters or to simply take care of yourself. This is bound to be a stressful time for you, so a little time off may be a good idea. That way, neither you nor your work will suffer.

Your teammate, if female, may choose to keep her ex-husband's name. She would then be addressed as Mrs. Sally Harrington or Ms. Sally Harrington. If she has taken back her maiden name, she is addressed as Ms. Sally Whitmore. The title of Miss is used only for women who have never been married.

She will need to send an e-mail or a memo to staff, the property's telephone operators, and anyone else who answers the telephones regarding her new name. No explanation is needed in the message. Simply state that the name has changed from this to that and they are being alerted since they receive incoming calls.

Make sure that business cards and telephone lists, both computer and paper, are updated. Make appropriate online and Website changes. Employees going through a divorce need to alert the human resources department of any name change for updating and record keeping purposes on health, life insurance, or other benefits.

If your associate is going through a separation, never ask questions. More important, never say anything at all about the spouse. Should the couple reconcile, you may not be remembered in a positive way.

SUICIDE

The tragedy of suicide generally leaves us speechless and unable to make sense of what happened. Should this sad situation happen to a family member or close friend of one of your associates, never pry and never ignore the situation. Offer your condolences. Let your friend know that you are aware of this difficult situation and are there for him or her.

GRACEFULLY EXITING YOUR JOB

There is nothing quite as shocking as being told that your position has been eliminated or that you are being fired. What's important is that you remain calm and listen very carefully. Do not become so upset that you fail to hear that you are being considered for another position or an internal transfer. If this was not said, then speak up and find out what the next step is. Ask for the assistance you need. If you were not trained properly or not given the tools you needed to do your job successfully, let your manager know in the kindest and most professional way that you can. Managers can make mistakes.

If the situation cannot be corrected, make sure that you exit like a professional. Let your manager know that, regardless of whatever happened, it was always nice working with him or her and the team. Never jeopardize the possibility of getting a good recommendation. Brand policy usually states that recommendations of any kind are not given. Don't believe it. People talk. Make sure they have something nice to say about you.

You will be told when your end date is. Be as professional as possible during this time. Find out from your human resources department about the insurance and other benefits you are able to take away with you. Never say anything negative about this private matter to the rest of the team. You might say, "Sometimes things happen. It's been a pleasure to work with you." If you are offered assistance in finding a new job, accept it. Should someone you know ever be in this situation, say something constructive like, "You know so much about operations. Other organizations will recognize this as soon as they meet you."

Should you decide to leave your position voluntarily, check your brand's policy regarding how much notice is expected. Policy may require that you submit a letter of resignation. No matter why you resigned, absolutely never say anything bad about your former employer to anyone. The industry is not that large. People know each other, and bad news travels quickly. I know it will be difficult, but be as gracious as you possibly can.

CHAPTER 5

Electronic Etiquette
Using Technology

What a wonderful and small world we now have thanks to technology. We use the Internet for research, education, entertainment, and instant communication. All office related technology, smartphones, tablets, voice mails, Web conferencing, and social networking are tremendous assets in business and in our personal lives. These excellent and time saving electronic tools developed so quickly that the rules of common sense and good manners just did not seem to keep up. The essential thing to remember about business manners is that it's all about kindness and putting others at ease. With that in mind, here goes.

E-MAIL

E-mail technology is best used for short and straightforward messages. Respond to all e-mails within twenty-four hours. Always assume that your e-mail is not private, will be seen by others, and lives permanently in your organization's computer backup system (server or cloud).

Once you hit the send button, that's it, so do not make the potentially costly mistake of viewing your business e-mails as casual correspondence. Here are the basic business writing and content guidelines for your work related e-mails:

- Know that someday your e-mails may be used as evidence in a prolonged and painful litigation experience.
- Don't even think about sending jokes or chain letters through your property's e-mail system, or anything intimidating, sexually harassing, religious, political, racially rude, or in any other way inappropriate.
- Check for spelling, correct capitalization, grammar, and tone; this is a business communication.
- Never write in all caps, as this means you are shouting. Forget the cute emoticons—they're not businesslike.
- Absolutely never use texting abbreviations in your business e-mails. This is a serious affront to your brand's reputation. You and your communication will not be taken seriously.

Also important are these basics of sending and copying:

- The "To" line is where you put the name of the person you mean to receive your message.
- The "Cc" is where you place the name of anyone else you want to know the content of the e-mail. If you expect a reply from those on the "Cc" line, then you need to move them to the "To" line.
- The "Bcc" line means blind copy. You are informing the "Bcc" person about the e-mail, but those on the "To" and "Cc" lines will not see this e-mail address. In other words, they will never know you have copied those on the "Bcc" line.

Make sure you have read and understood your brand's e-mail policy. Don't just assume that the client, associate, or guest actually received your e-mail. Things happen. E-mail servers can go down, or your e-mail may be addressed incorrectly and never reach the intended recipient.

Should you receive a receipt saying the e-mail was read, remember that this may or may not be so. It can't hurt to follow up with guests and fellow associates, as appropriate, with a telephone call, written note, or personal visit. Nothing in cyberspace will ever replace the warmth of the in person human experience.

CELL PHONES AND PAGERS

One night, while dining at a local Asian restaurant, I watched as the four university students at the next table all used their cell phones simultaneously and continuously. I kept wondering why they were bothering to have dinner together. It certainly wasn't to talk to each other. They did not know that the most important people in the world are the ones directly in front of them at any time. They looked unschooled in basic manners. They looked rude. I wonder how well they will do fitting in at their first jobs.

It's very important in business that you not answer your cell phone unless you are in a position to have a conversation. And remember not to use your cell phone to conduct company business in an elevator or in any public place. You are holding the rest of us hostage in the elevator while we listen to what you have to say. Also, we all find it annoying that your cell phone ring plays "Hail to the Chief."

Do I have to say it? Please stop using your cell phone in public restrooms. As in an elevator, you are holding the rest of us hostage to your conversation. More to the point, why would you make a personal or a business telephone call when all around you water is running and toilets are flushing?

The following are general guidelines for public and business cell phone usage:

- The protocol for public cell phone usage is to keep a distance of ten feet between you and the nearest person.
- In business, your cell phone or pager should always be set on vibrate. It should never ring in the middle of a meeting, in your cubicle or office, in an elevator, or in front of your guest.

- Answer your business cell phone professionally using both your first and last names. Business telephone calls are to the point; they are brief. Return messages within twenty-four hours.
- When you are having a conversation on your cell phone, never speak with anyone who is standing near you. This would be rude to the person with whom you are already having a conversation.
- Never ignore an in person guest while you are speaking on your cell phone. Accomplish this by never speaking on your cell phone in any of the guest areas of your property or company.
- Never initiate or answer a telephone call from a restaurant table or during a business meeting. This code of behavior holds true in your social life as well.

To be heard and understood when using a cell phone, please speak clearly and slowly, and no "cell yell." If you are at a business meal or in a colleague's office and your cell phone vibrates, excuse yourself and step outside of the room to take the call.

When you're not at work, the following cell phone guidelines apply:

- Do not speak on your cell phone in doctors' and dentists' offices, hospital waiting rooms, at movies, at live performances, or at funerals.
- Do not speak on your cell phone while waiting in line at the bank or the deli, or while in a museum or library. You may wish to check your e-mails and text messages or search the Web instead.
- Never speak on your cell phone in any covered public space.
- If you absolutely must use your cell phone on a train or on a bus, please keep your voice very low and your conversation brief.

If you drive as part of your hospitality role, I strongly recommend that you do not use your cell phone while driving on business unless it is for your own or someone else's personal safety. Ask your risk manager or human resources director for a copy of your organization's policy regarding speaking on the cell phone while driving on company business. Some policies allow for the use of a headset, earbuds, or a hands-free mounted system for cell phones. Others do not.

Pagers are being issued less frequently; but, if you are issued a pager, cell phone protocols are followed. Pagers are never placed on a dining table, a conference table, or on your client's, guest's, or associate's desk. Please keep the pager set on vibrate and answer the page outside of your meetings and away from public areas.

This is mentioned in the section called "Smartphones and Tablets," but it is worth repeating: never place your cell phone on a potential client's desk.

WEARABLE TECHNOLOGY

Google has created a wearable computer called "Glass." Glass looks and fits like modern eyeglasses that have a small clear screen over one eye. Glass displays information exactly like a hands-free smartphone. The wearer interacts with the Internet through voice commands and can scroll through data with a tilt of the head. There is a touchpad by the wearer's ear. Glass has a camera and can record video (Wikipedia 2014). Since this device can record live events, wearers have been banned from some movie theaters, restaurants and casinos. There are also security and privacy concerns (as with smartphones) when considering the possibility of sensitive brand, guest, and employee information that can be recorded. Glass is being used in some hospitals so that physicians can quickly call up patient information (Borchers 2014).

Other companies are marketing smartwatches with touch screens. Apple's product is the iWatch. Wearable computer technology is also made for the fitness, sports, and virtual reality markets. This technology will be used on the field and in the gym and locker room. Issues of brand, guest, and employee privacy are major concerns.

A Bluetooth wireless earpiece is a hands-free telephone that the user wears in his or her ear. These are excellent devices when used in call centers and in any telephone intensive job. The user has his or her hands free while having telephone conversations.

A MP3 player and an iPod are examples of portable media players. If your organization allows you to use a media player so that you can enjoy music while you work, remove both of your earbuds (or your headset) when you are speaking, in person, with a coworker.

Remove your Bluetooth wireless earpiece, or Glass when speaking with a person who is standing right in front of you. Do not wear these devices during business meetings. Do not wear them at either a business or a social meal. If you are wearing a smartwatch, refrain from looking at it during your business meal.

Never enter a business meeting using any of these devices. You will not look prepared, and most certainly you will send the message that the meeting is not as important as your telephone conversation or data search. Finish your conversation or Internet search in the hall before entering the meeting and remember to remove any distracting wireless devices.

Don't even think about wearing a wireless earpiece, Glass, or a headset in the public areas of your property. Visible earbuds, cell phones, and other communication devices, tell your guests that you are not focused on their needs. As with a cell phone, it is rude to use your wireless device in an elevator. Never use your wireless devices to conduct brand business in any public place.

When you are not at work, remember that these same rules of consideration regarding this technology apply to your time spent in a house of worship or at a movie, play, or symphony. This technology should never be placed on a dining or conference table. With all technology, ask permission before taking pictures or recording.

TEXT MESSAGING AND TWEETING

The same protocol for cell phones applies to text messaging and tweeting. Text messaging, or texting, is an exchange of short business or social messages between people on their mobile phones. Twitter is a social networking service that lets users send and read short messages (up to 140 characters) in real time. The messages, or updates, are known as *tweets.*

No texting or tweeting (sometimes called *twittering*) from restaurants, meetings, seminars, movie theaters, or houses of worship. In a dim auditorium, even the speaker can see the warm glow of your texting, and those around you may hear the dull tap, tap, tap. Sadly, you will appear rude and uninformed if you check your text messages during a business setting.

In the "Meeting Etiquette" section of chapter 2, I advised you to never walk into a business meeting while checking your text messages or your e-mails. Since you are being watched (and judged) when you enter a room, why not enter a room smiling, looking confident, prepared, and approachable?

The term *textual harassment* refers to sending inappropriate text messages that may lead to claims of various types of workplace harassment (such as sexual, racial, or religious harassment). I am fairly confident that I do not need to discuss the perils of texting and tweeting while driving. Ask your human resources representative if a texting policy is in place for your brand.

CELL PHONE CAMERAS

The exceptional technology of the cell phone can easily be misused. Many brands have strict policies regarding camera usage. Only use your camera at work if digital pictures are needed for a project or to record an associate's milestone, accomplishment, or other work related celebration.

Always ask permission before taking a coworker's picture. It should go without saying that you will never take a picture of a guest. Celebrities and people from all walks of life stay, fly, and cruise with you and you don't want to invade a guest's privacy or mishandle the trust he or she has placed in your brand.

Sensitive corporate and guest information, employee Social Security numbers, and other identifying information have been photographed/copied and stolen using cell phone cameras and other technology like flash drives; this is called *slurping*. A flash drive is a data storage device with a very small memory. It is about the size of a thumb and is sometimes called a thumb drive.

Unless they are needed for your work, you may be better off just leaving your cell phone and other electronic devices in your briefcase. Carefully review your brand's policy regarding not only cell phone camera use but all other types of camera and video device use at your place of work.

PUSH-TO-TALK PHONES

Push-to-talk, or direct-connect, phones allow the caller to press a button and immediately be connected with someone who has the same telephone service. Originally, these were called walkie-talkie phones. These phones chirp, and anyone can hear both sides of your conversation. You can either turn the speaker off or keep your voice very low when using this distracting device. These telephones are excellent when used by medical emergency services personnel and on construction sites (Mitchell 2004). Other than in situations where speed is of the essence, I tend to think of this technology as useful mainly when playing war games.

VOICE MAIL

Your outgoing message is a professional statement of who you are, your name, your title, and the name of your property or organization. Speak *s-l-o-w-l-y*. Update your message should you plan to be out of the office.

When you leave a business voice mail for a guest or an associate, keep it brief and let the individual know how and when he or she can reach you. Even if you believe the person who called has your telephone number, or you know that his or her smartphone will have a record of the number, leave a return number anyway. Speak s-l-o-w-l-y. This is not a race.

SPEAKERPHONES

There is only one thing to remember about speakerphones: all privacy is lost. Let the person you've called (or the person who has called you) know that you wish to use the speakerphone and ask for his or her permission to do so. Identify, by name, each person who is in the room.

CONFERENCE CALLS

The conference call is a great way to get a number of people together efficiently. Generally, one person will manually connect the group by pressing the conference button for each single connection. Other systems require you to participate by calling a central number and/or by entering a password.

Identify yourself when you join a call. There may be a delay, so be careful not to speak over anyone. Think of the participants as being in the room with you. Never unwrap food or carry on conversations with someone else when on a conference call. We can all hear you.

FAX MACHINES

All of the information regarding e-mail business etiquette applies to the use of fax (facsimile) machines. All information that you believe to be confidential can be seen by anyone who walks by the receiving machine. Always call the recipient in advance so that he or she can intercept the fax. Remember that just because you receive a receipt that the fax went through does not mean that the intended recipient actually received your fax.

SMARTPHONES AND TABLETS

Using a smartphone or tablet is of great assistance for the busy hospitality associate. The problem is in the *when* and *where* of their use. There is a big difference between private and business usage. Privately, these electronics are great while waiting in line at the bank or riding the subway. You can check and send e-mails. You can surf the Internet (Zunk 2012).

In business, apply the same cell phone protocols to smartphone and tablet usage. You would never send a text message or check your e-mail while at a business meeting or in front of your associates, guests, family, or friends.

As mentioned earlier in the section on "Meeting Etiquette," your smartphone or tablet should never be placed on a dining or conference table. The only time that a smartphone, tablet, or laptop is ever placed on a conference table is when you are using it to give a presentation, to show your clients or associates a project related item, or to take notes during a meeting. Never use electronics to check your e-mails, texts, or surf the Web during a business meeting.

Remember that the living, breathing person in front of you is much more important than your electronic devices. Please don't use your smartphone or tablet while at the movies. The light is distracting to the rest of us.

INSTANT MESSAGES (IMS)

Unlike e-mailing, instant messaging is a real time conversation between at least two people through computers. In business, instant messages (IMs) may seem casual; but in the context of your work, they are professional communications.

The IM is an unexpected interruption to the receiver. Start your message by asking if this is a good time to chat. If it's not, then log off.

Treat IMs exactly like e-mails. You are representing your brand, and your instant messaging conversations are not private. They can be retrieved, so keep your words and tone businesslike (Bremer 2004b).

TELEPHONE MANNERS

The protocol for landline usage is the same as for cellular telephones. The person in front of you is the most important person at that moment. If you are visiting an associate's office and he or she must answer a business line, offer to leave and return at another time.

Most brands want telephones answered within three rings. Try to use your guest's name whenever you can. Never screen a call by saying, "Let me check if he is in" or "May I tell him who is calling?" If the caller wants to speak with Mr. Wong, you will say, "Of course. It's my pleasure. May I tell him who is calling?" If you are the caller, you can simplify matters by always stating your name (and, if appropriate, your title) before requesting to speak with a colleague or guest.

Being transferred from department to department may infuriate your guests. Eliminate call transfers if you can. Depending on the purpose of the call, your caller may be losing his or her patience. Find the correct answer yourself, even if it means having to say, "Mr. Casey, I will find the correct answer to your question. May I please call you back in a few minutes?" If it will be longer than a few minutes, let the guest know this.

Limit personal calls received and made at the office to emergencies and very important matters only (on both your cell phone and office line). I am confident that you know to avoid eating or chewing gum while speaking on the telephone.

Answering Someone Else's Telephone

Answer a colleague's office line by saying, "Good morning, this is Michael Broadmeadow's office. My name is Edwin Stephens; how may I assist you?" The caller will probably want to speak with Mr. Broadmeadow. Write down the caller's name (verify correct spelling), telephone number, and purpose for the call. Note the day and the time of the call. Then be sure that Mr. Broadmeadow actually gets the message.

If you are able to take care of the matter, note this on the pad or message slip, or let your colleague know this electronically by e-mail or text. Have you promised a follow-up call? Either you or the person the caller was trying to reach must follow through. Let your associate know right away that a guest is trying to reach him or her. In your own office, always have a pad and a pen sitting right by your telephone.

Learn the customs and expectations of your department. Are you expected to answer the business line of a superior? Find out.

Receiving Calls in a Language You Do Not Speak

This topic has the distinction of making both parties uncomfortable and sometimes frustrated. The hospitality industry, by its very nature, invites the entire world to telephone your property. Be prepared. Get a friend to write these words in the language of your choice: "My _____ is not very good. I will find someone to assist you. May I please place you on hold? Thank you very much." Practice pronouncing your speech correctly. Keep this memo by your telephone. Keep it in your pocket.

Keeping and Being Kept on Hold

Never keep anyone on hold for more than one minute. If you must place the caller on hold to resolve or research the matter, ask permission: "May I place you on a brief hold?" Thank the caller when you resume the conversation.

If it took a little longer than expected, say, "I'm sorry that took longer than expected. Thank you for your patience. You'll be happy to hear that I found that special gourmet dog food for Mr. Fido."

If you are placed on hold for more than three minutes, you may hang up the telephone. When you call back, tell the listener you were unable to continue to hold.

If Disconnected, Who Calls Back?

If you are disconnected, it does not matter who placed the call. In business, you, not the customer or guest, always call back. Socially, the person who placed the call should call back.

Ending the Call

The rule is that the person who initiated the telephone call is the person who is supposed to terminate the call. Since this may or may not happen, when the business seems complete, you must say, "I'm glad we were able to resolve this so quickly. Is there anything else I may assist you with?" Carefully place the telephone receiver into its base. Your guest or other caller may still be on the line, and you do not want him or her to hear the receiver being slammed down.

Wrong Numbers

When you dial a wrong number, admit it and apologize. Let the listener know what number you were trying to reach. This way, that person can let you know exactly where you went wrong, and neither of you will be annoyed with another misdialed telephone call. Just say, "I'm so sorry to have bothered you; I've misdialed. I was trying to reach 854-2351." Please don't just hang up when you know you've made a mistake. Should someone dial you by mistake, offer him or her the same courtesy: "You've misdialed. That's all right."

Call-Waiting

Call-waiting is the only electronic telephone feature that allows you to insult two callers at the same time! You tell the first caller to hold because there may be someone more important on the other line. Then you insult caller number two by saying, "I can't talk because someone else is more important. I only picked up the line to tease you." By the time you get back to caller number one, any glow that the relationship had is over. When you are on a call with a client or guest, have your incoming calls forwarded to voice mail or to the receptionist or other colleague.

If a guest calls while you are waiting for another guest's call, tell the first guest that you are expecting an interruption to this conversation. Ask if you may give him or her your undivided attention in a few minutes. If the guest agrees, go on with the conversation until it is interrupted. Then you must apologize: "I'm so sorry Mrs. Chang, this is the interruption I told you about. May I meet you in the lobby in fifteen minutes to continue our discussion?"

Caller ID

Caller ID has all of the properties of a double-edged sword. If you answer with the caller's name one day and the next you do not pick up, then on day two the caller may think that you are avoiding him or her. You may actually be out of the office.

My suggestion is that you use caller ID to assist you in being prepared to take the call (grabbing the right file or scrolling through your database to find an answer). Never answer with, "Hello, Sam." This can be off-putting. The only time you will properly answer your office telephone with the caller's name is if he or she is a guest who is calling from a guest room and the room is identified by your property's telephone system.

Public Telephones

Public telephones, also called pay phones, are lifesavers when traveling. Your cell phone may not work when you are out of your network's area. Purchase a calling card. With this prepaid telephone card, you will be able to use a pay telephone at most locations worldwide. Even if you have a cell phone, it's a good idea to have a prepaid card with you on business trips, just in case.

Make sure the pay phone you are using is in a well lighted, public area. Make your call quickly. If you are waiting to use a public pay phone, please don't stand inappropriately close to the person who is ahead of you. If you are truly having an emergency or must meet a deadline, politely say to the person ahead of you, "Sir, I have an emergency call to make, can you help me? I'll only be a minute." Say thank you and keep your promise.

THE INTERNET

Use the World Wide Web positively. Cyberspace civility at work necessitates your use of the same courtesies and common sense that you would use anywhere else on your property. Whatever messages you send out and whatever Websites you view on your business computer, laptop, tablet, smartphone, or any other electronic device are not private. These electronic tools at work were never meant for personal use. Many employers monitor Internet usage. Put simply, no Web surfing unless it is for business purposes.

Imagine how sad and embarrassing it would be if you sent out an intolerant or otherwise unacceptable message and your company discovered this, or if you visit either an adult Website or a site that is ethically inappropriate and you are discovered. If you receive inappropriate messages on your computer, smartphone, tablet, or business related social network, you will need to immediately report it to both your supervisor and the information technology department. Never open a questionable e-mail or link, as computer viruses are a significant business concern.

Social Networking

Social networking Websites are inexpensive and accessible to anyone. They are sites used to publish or access all kinds of information. You might use a social networking Website to advertise a brand or to exchange ideas, or you may wish to let family and friends know about some special event in your life. Some brands encourage positive use of your experience at work while others discourage your using the brand's name on social networking sites. Find out from your human resources department what your brand's social networking policy is.

Facebook is the world's largest social networking Website. It is used to connect to family, friends, and business associates. Users create a profile page that gives personal and professional information and shows photographs. Typically, everyone within the user's network can view all information posted and can post comments of his or her own. Many businesses have a presence on Facebook and other social networking sites to promote their brands. LinkedIn is a business oriented, social networking service. It is the largest professional networking platform on the Web. Users look for professional opportunities and share career related insights with colleagues on LinkedIn.

Another excellent social networking site is Tango, an all-in-one social networking application that allows you to interact with clients, friends, and family. You can send free text messages, make free telephone and video calls, and play games.

Remember that nothing is private on the Internet. Employment recruiters, when checking an applicant's Web presence, will carefully examine what is posted on Facebook, LinkedIn, and other sites. As a professional, you may not want to post a picture of yourself in a bar, drinking and celebrating your birthday with your friends.

Video-Sharing Websites

Photo-sharing services like Instagram and Snapchat let users take pictures and videos (using their cell phones or tablets) and share them on social networks like Facebook, Twitter, Tumblr, Flickr, and WhatsApp Messenger. WhatsApp Messenger is also an excellent texting platform. Clients, friends, family, and strangers worldwide have access to comments, pictures, videos, and audio media messages. Some sites allow the user to block adult or inappropriate material. Others do not.

YouTube

YouTube is a video-sharing Website that has a worldwide reach. People post videos on YouTube. The videos can be fun, educational, commercial, or personal in nature. Other people may post their opinions about the videos. You can post a résumé, advertise a new business, or search for a husband. YouTube is a useful tool in news media, entertainment, business, and even politics.

Keep in mind that things may not always be as they seem in an online community. Whatever is posted on the Internet lasts forever and is seen by millions of people. Potential employers may see what you have posted. Make sure that you are proud of the items you post about yourself. Check your brand's policy regarding using the brand's name on video-sharing Websites.

Web Conferencing

Web conferencing is a sort of online conference room. It enables people at different locations to meet at the same time, online. Teams in different cities and countries can work, share ideas and information, or take part in a training seminar. Interviews and sales presentations can be conducted via Web conferencing. FaceTime, Skype, WebEx, and GoToMeeting are popular web conferencing sites.

During a Web conference, you have an opportunity to appear calm and professional or to look like a real mess! There might be a slight delay between sound and motion in Web conferencing. Be careful not to talk over someone else. Just look at the monitor and remember that this is not like speaking on your cell phone. Participants can watch as you slouch, roll your eyes, scratch an itch, or cross your legs in a less than professional manner. Think of the other conference participants as sitting right across from you. Take this opportunity to connect in a positive way with your colleagues.

Blogs

A blog is a running commentary of opinions and creative ideas. Some, written by one or two authors, function as personal online diaries. Others are used for online brand advertising. Company blogs are used as marketing and public relations tools. Countless businesses have company sponsored blogs to enable employees, guests, and clients to learn about the organization and its special offers; to compliment associates; and to announce new products. Multi-author blogs are written by a large number of authors. They may be professionally edited. Readers of both personal and business blogs leave comments in an interactive format.

Electronic Mailing Lists

Electronic mailing lists are kept by companies and other organizations for sending out e-mails to members, customers, guests, and subscribers. The lists are used for widespread distribution of messages, and each message on an electronic list is sent to all list members. LISTSERV is one example of an electronic mailing list.

Your comments on such a list are automatically broadcast to everyone on the list. Your words become a part of a larger forum of comments. Think carefully when adding your written thoughts to such a forum. Nothing is as private as it seems in cyberspace.

Podcasts

Podcasts are essentially radio programs that can be posted on your brand's Website. Anyone with a microphone or even a telephone can create a podcast. Blog Talk Radio (a talk radio and podcast hosting platform) and similar services allow people to call in and create a podcast. You can listen to podcasts with any computer, tablet, or smartphone that is connected to the Internet. You can play podcasts on your computer or download them to your tablet, iPad, or other MP3 player. An MP3 player is a portable audio device, and generally an image viewing device as well.

There are podcasts about knitting, eye surgery, and world peace. The possibilities are endless. Your brand may offer outstanding hard and soft skills training programs and informational brand forums and industry related guest speakers through podcasts. Podcasts are wonderful educational tools. You can tune into company sponsored training sessions at your own convenience by downloading the training from your brand's Website to your laptop, tablet, or MP3 player.

MP3 players, while placing you closer to your music and other information, tune out the rest of us. Of course, you will never use your MP3 player on property unless you are having lunch by yourself.

Podcasts can be very public. Should you participate in a podcast that is not sponsored by your brand, never mention the name of your brand. Check your company's policy on podcasting. If a policy on this or any electronic technology topic does not exist, suggest to the human resources department that it be created in the best interests of the organization.

INFORMATION SECURITY

You probably signed a paper at your orientation that said you would not share company information with outsiders. Information is found everywhere: paper documents, flash drives, smartphones, and more. If you are not taking these and other sensitive items with you during the day, lock them up when you leave your office or when you leave for the evening. Be mindful of where you leave your laptop, smartphone, notepad or tablet. Always back up your work. Do this often.

CHAPTER 6

Business Travel
Travel Essentials

Business travel can be exhilarating for the new hospitality management associate. You are well thought of or you would not have been chosen for the assignment. Now the question is, "What do I do?" This is easy. Just plan well, arrive everywhere early, and take extra money (lots of dollar bills).

In your wallet, you may have credit cards, an employee picture ID, a driver's license, an ATM (automatic teller machine) card, a health insurance card, traveler's checks, and other needed cards with essential information. Photocopy these cards (front and back) along with your traveler's checks and place these copies in your carry-on tote or other carry-on luggage. Leave an extra copy at home. If your handbag or wallet is stolen, repairing the damage in an unfamiliar city or foreign country will be much easier.

Make sure that your cell phone has been fully charged and that your cell phone charger and an extra battery are in your carry-on bag. I know you keep important telephone numbers in your cell phone contact list, but take a paper list of needed telephone numbers and addresses with you just in case your phone dies. Bring a prepaid phone card. Most important: practice patience and expect the unexpected.

PACKING WISELY

Whenever possible, limit your luggage to your carry-on tote or briefcase (or computer bag) and a small rolling piece of luggage (or a garment bag). You may have to spend considerable time running to catch your connecting flights or the parking garage bus. You will have to cart your own suitcases around airports and rental car lots looking for your lost metallic blue rental car. Whenever you check luggage, you do run the risk of your clothes having a wonderful vacation in Mexico City while you arrive in Europe without your pants.

Carry the following on board with you:

- prescriptions, contact lenses and glasses, cell phone, traveler's checks, credit cards, camera, and laptop
- essential toiletries (in unbreakable containers that conform to airline requirements)
- any undergarments you may need should your luggage be delayed a day or two
- business shoes, since you are probably traveling in airport friendly shoes that aren't appropriate in a business situation
- whatever cash, jewelry, or other valuables you're bringing— they should never go in checked luggage
- a small calculator if you are going out of the country, so you can convert currency and perhaps mileage

When packing electronics for your business trip, remember your cell phone and charger, an extra cell phone battery, and any adapter that may be necessary for your electronics. An adapter is a device that adapts the electric current of the country you are visiting to conform to the electric current your device requires. Don't bother bringing a hair dryer, as all good hotels have them. E-mail your concierge in advance and ask about needed amenities and the use of electronics in your host country.

Since this is a business trip, travel in a business suit like I do. You just may get an upgrade if you look professional. More to the point, if your luggage is delayed, you will still be ready to give a speech or attend a seminar. For longer flights, you may wish to pack a suit in your carry-on instead of arriving wrinkled. Consider the following when packing your suitcase:

- Good travel fabrics are wrinkle-resistant wools and gabardines. Crepe is a good summer travel fabric. Avoid thick garments.
- Try to stay with one or two basic colors. Black, navy, or taupe/cream/tan garments can be matched with almost all other colors.
- Lay out what you plan to take well in advance of your trip so that you can see what else you may need. Don't forget to lay out your shoe choices and other accessories (belts, ties, jewelry, cuff links, scarves) so that nothing essential is forgotten.
- Take an extra shirt in a neutral color even if you are only going to be away for one or two days. Spills, ink, ketchup, and who knows what else are always just waiting out there for you.
- Remember to pack an appropriate garment(s) for your off time. Appropriate garments for both business and relaxed outings will be determined by the country you are visiting. In some countries, women are required to be more covered (longer skirts and long-sleeved garments).
- Both men and women need to research appropriate business and casual dress for the region they will be visiting.
- Check the weather in advance, by Internet or by calling the hotel's concierge several days in advance of the trip. You may need an all-weather trench coat or boots.

- Your hotel may be able to efficiently launder items for you. If you are staying at a motel, there may be a washer and dryer for you to use.
- Don't count on a washer or dryer. Always pack extra undergarments.

Airport Security Lines

Be prepared. Have your ticket or boarding pass, picture ID, and passport (if required) easily accessible.

Checking Luggage

Use Transportation Security Administration (TSA) locks. These locks allow airport security personnel to efficiently open your checked luggage with a master key without damaging either your lock or your suitcase. These locks have a color indicator to show whether or not your bag has been opened and inspected. A green indicator means your luggage has been opened; red means it has not. Purchase TSA locks in advance at any luggage or hardware store. They are also sold at airport luggage shops.

If you see that your bag has been opened, do a quick on the spot check of your belongings. If anything is missing or damaged, report this to the airport security department while you are still at the airport.

For insurance purposes, keep a list of all items that you check, in case of loss. Always put your business address on luggage tags. Do not put your home address on your luggage tag. For safety reasons, no one has to know where you live. Because luggage tags can be lost, tape a business card inside each piece of luggage, whether the piece is checked or not.

COMMERCIAL AIR

First and most important, did you remember to take your ticket/ boarding pass, picture ID, and passport, if required? You will be boarding by row or section based on where you are sitting.

This is where your patience may be tried. To be a good passenger, remember the following:

- Be careful that your carry-on bags don't knock a fellow passenger unconscious.
- Once on board, quickly put away your bags and get out of the aisle. Pretend that you are at work with your wonderful coworkers. Smile at airline personnel.
- Say hello to your row mates; nod and smile.
- Be respectful regarding working on the plane. Make sure that your laptop and paperwork are not in your neighbor's lap.
- If you are seated next to Chatty Cathy, just say, "Please excuse me, I need to work now." Remember to smile.
- Never wear perfume on an airplane. This is a very small space and there is generally enough sneezing, wheezing, and coughing going on.
- Everyone, as a matter of common courtesy, please remove your hats, caps, and hoodies in this enclosed public space.

In the "Packing Wisely" section of this chapter, I mention that, when on business, I always travel in a business suit and pack needed essentials and toiletries in my tote just in case my checked luggage is delayed. When traveling to a speaking engagement, I mail seminar handouts to the location ahead of time, or I take them with me in carry-on luggage. Never check needed materials or your laptop.

Most important, take along a snack of your choice. Even if you are flying first or business class, you just never know how much time you may spend waiting on a runway and whether or not you will be offered anything to eat or drink.

The following tips apply to overseas flights and cross country flights:

- In first and business class, you may have a seat that can be tilted back into a bed.

- Make sure that the passenger seated directly behind you is not eating or about to take a sip of hot coffee when you decide to recline your seat.
- If you are traveling coach, try to book an aisle seat that has an empty middle seat next to it.
- The bulkhead seats and those next to the emergency exits have the most leg room.
- If you sit by an emergency exit, it will be your duty to open this door if required to do so after an emergency landing. Make sure that you wish to and are physically able to do so should you take this roomy seat.

On all flights, remember the following:

- You or your travel agent must book your seat well in advance of your trip so that you will be as comfortable as possible.
- You do not want to wind up in a middle seat or in a nonreclining seat.
- In a nonreclining seat, you will not be as comfortable as you could be.
- The nonreclining seats are usually found in the back of the plane, near the restrooms.
- Sitting near the restrooms means that you will be subjected to a constant parade of fellow passengers waiting in line to use a toilet. They will be waiting directly next to your seat.

CORPORATE JET

Lucky you! You've been invited to travel on your organization's corporate jet. Dress professionally; think of this trip as an important business day. Arrive early. If everyone is there, the pilot may be able to take off early. You don't want to be the person keeping everyone else waiting. Corporate jets are often leased by the hour. If you're late, you not only cost your company money, but I am fairly certain that you will not be invited back. The basics of corporate jet travel include the following:

- You will have to make your own travel arrangements getting to and from the airport.
- Let your senior executives board first. Wait until your senior executives are seated before choosing your own seat, or wait for a crew member to seat you. Senior executives get the best seats.
- Some corporate jets have a steward on board. If not, you will get your own food and beverages.
- Bring your used plates, glasses, cups, napkins, and silverware back to the galley. The galley is the kitchen area.
- Your seating area should be left in the same clean and orderly condition in which you found it.
- On your business flight, do not ask for a magazine or a newspaper. Come prepared with your own reading material. If this is a working flight, do not take out a book or e-reader. Follow the lead of your senior personnel.

Be mindful of your brand's policy regarding alcohol during working hours. Never ask for an alcoholic beverage. If an executive opens a bottle of wine (or other alcoholic beverage) and offers a glass to each member of the group, then you may be comfortable in joining your colleagues.

Take only your carry-on tote or briefcase (or computer bag) and a small rolling piece of luggage (or a garment bag). Not only will you be expected to carry your own suitcases, but you will be unable to take a lot of luggage on a small jet.

Check with the person who made these travel arrangements for you. He or she will answer questions about your luggage or anything else related to your flight. Don't forget to write a thank-you note to this helpful associate. Please remember to thank the steward, the pilot, and the copilot by name for a wonderful flight. Remember that it's *pilot* not *captain* on a private jet.

Should you be offered a ride (that does not involve business) on the private jet of a friend, it is appropriate to bring a gift of food that can be enjoyed during the flight

HELICOPTER

Generally, an organization owns a helicopter if executives need a quick way to get around a large city, avoiding drive time traffic. Large cities are likely to have buildings with rooftop landing pads. It may be that the chief executive uses the helicopter to get to and from work or to arrive on time at important meetings. If you are asked to join company executives on the helicopter, dress professionally. Under no circumstances will you ever ask a top executive if you can hitch a ride on the helicopter.

SHIP

You may be traveling by ship for a company event, seminar, or convention. You may be traveling with senior personnel, so make sure to arrive at least three or four hours before your ship is scheduled to leave. You do not want to inconvenience your group by being late and causing everyone to stand endlessly in a long line.

As at an airport, you will need to have your identification, tickets, and other paperwork ready and easily accessible. Make sure that your luggage is tagged on the outside. As with air travel, I always tape my business card on the inside of my luggage just in case the outside tag is lost. Your entire group will need to fill out customs forms and boarding passes; bring both pens and patience (Ingram 2005).

Get a diagram of the ship from your travel agent, or from the Web, well in advance. Pack light, because space on a ship is very limited and because you may have to do some serious carrying of your luggage up ramps or stairways when boarding. Additionally, you may be returning home by air, and you'll want to have fewer (and lighter) pieces of luggage to handle at the airport.

Dress appropriately for the scheduled events. Your travel agent and the cruise line will be able to advise you if there will be a formal night during your cruise. The formal night is an evening on board when all passengers dress up for a more elegant dining experience. Day wear is very casual. On the ocean, the tropics can be chilly at night. Even on the most casual cruise, it makes sense for men to bring a jacket along and for women to bring a light sweater, summer jacket, or shawl.

Don't leave your business manners back on shore. This may be a training or celebratory event, but never forget that your senior management is watching and that they have invested time, attention, and money in you. You have worked hard to be able to attend this seminar or event.

Address officers by their correct titles, such as captain. Watch your dining and drinking behavior. Behave with decorum at the buffet and at all onboard entertainment. Now relax and enjoy.

YACHT

Should your client or guest invite you onto his or her yacht, there are two important things to remember. The first is that the owner is the first one to board the vessel and the last one to leave. The second is that a yacht is referred to as *she*.

The owner of a yacht often employs a skipper (or captain) who is responsible not only for the boat but for the safety of everyone on board. This person is the boss. Do what he or she tells you to do. Do not get comfortable until the skipper tells you where to sit. Never speak to or distract the skipper while he or she is docking the boat.

Always board the yacht in rubber soled shoes unless you are told otherwise. Clothing must be appropriate, so speak with your host to make sure that you will be dressed correctly for the occasion. Remember to take any medicine for seasickness before you board so that your sail will be pleasant (Grotts 2009). As you would do as a guest in a private home, it is correct to bring a hostess gift to the yacht. A bottle of Champagne is always appropriate. A handwritten thank-you note is mandatory.

TRAIN

When doing business in Europe, you will surely travel by rail at some point. At the station, you will purchase your ticket either at a freestanding booth or at a train station window. Each will be clearly marked for ticket sales.

Train travel protocol means queuing up (getting in line) to wait for the train's arrival. Queuing is also practiced on the Continent when waiting for buses. It's a wonderfully civilized custom. You must get into line behind those who arrived at the depot before you. When the train pulls into the station, all travelers exit the railcars and then those who are waiting in the queue may enter the railcars in an orderly fashion.

Where you sit depends on your ticket. There are both first class and coach seating areas on European commuter trains. In North America, when traveling long distances by rail, there are three levels of seating: first class, business class, and coach.

If you are traveling overnight on a train and have a sleeping car, you still may not have a private bathroom. If this is the case, make sure that you bring a robe along. It is perfectly proper to wear your robe in the aisles to and from the bathroom, even if you do bump into your boss. This is a business trip, however, so make sure that the robe has adequate coverage in terms of both fabric and length. Use the facility quickly and leave it clean for other passengers. You may want to ask your sleeping car attendant to wake you up in the morning (Mitchell 2004).

For other than commuter trains, you can always find food in the dining car. Prepared foods are always for sale in coach. There may even be a bistro or a bar car on your train. On any type of train, remember to speak softly if you are using a cell phone. If I am sitting next you, I promise that I will find your conversation annoying.

The mantra of "be kind" applies as well. Help others who need assistance in heaving bags into an overhead rack or storage compartment. Collect your own candy wrappers and water bottles. If you are not ill or disabled, give up your commuter seat to an elderly person or to someone who is profoundly pregnant, ill, or disabled. Have your ticket out and be really nice to the conductor. His or her job can't be easy.

On all trains, if you are carrying tote bags, backpacks, umbrellas, or luggage, please stow them. On commuter trains, you will not be able to place your handbag, computer case, shaving kit, or skateboard on the seat next to you. Just as on an airplane, make sure that your laptop and paperwork are not in your neighbor's lap.

BUS

The protocol for bus travel is similar to rail travel. Whether on business or not, it is best not to bring onion and sardine sandwiches or any other malodorous foods onboard. These are close quarters. I recommend that you bring with you your iPod, tablet, earbuds, and/or a book. Your seatmates will frown on loud cell phone conversations and rings that play the theme song from *The Titanic*.

You will want to dress comfortably, if this is other than a quick in town business trip. As on a ship and an airplane, luggage is usually limited to two pieces per passenger. On commercial bus lines, you do not tip the driver. Think of your driver as the captain of his or her own ship.

Since there are no assigned seats on a bus, if you want to sleep, arrive early so that you can slump comfortably into a window seat. Be polite to fellow travelers by not kicking the seat in front of you. As on a commuter train, if this is a commuter bus and you are not yourself disabled or ill, give up your seat to an elderly person or to someone who is obviously pregnant, ill, or disabled.

RENTAL CAR

The senior members of your party may ask you to handle the rental car arrangements. I always call the actual location where I will be renting the car. There can be differences in rates and availability upon arrival if you depend on the national reservation center instead of the local folks. Also check the car rental rates online, as they are very often lower. Should you book online, follow up to confirm with the location where you are picking up your car.

Check with your accounting department regarding how you will pay for the car. You may be using your own credit card and obtaining reimbursement after the trip. The accounting department may want you to use a company credit card. Save your rental contract and all receipts. Check your organization's policy regarding whether you are to obtain additional accident insurance through the rental company.

Take with you the name and telephone number of the person at the local rental desk. This is the person with whom you actually made the arrangements. Specify if the car is to be nonsmoking or if you need a particularly large car or a van. On your way to return the car, fill it up with gas if you are not running late. Otherwise, the rental company will do this for you and may charge a very steep rate for gasoline. Check the rental car company's gasoline policy before your trip.

Seat the highest ranking member of your party in the front passenger seat. If you are traveling with clients, the client sits in the front passenger seat. Courtesy dictates that no one in your party smokes in the rental car. Make all cell phone calls before you enter your party's rental car. After that, it's best to wait until you've reached your destination to use your cell phone. In close quarters, cell phone rings, text messaging taps, and other repetitive noises will be very annoying.

TAXICAB

When you are hailing a taxicab at an airport or train station, there is usually a line of cabs waiting to pick up passengers. Get in line behind those travelers already waiting for a cab. Take the taxi that pulls up when it's your turn. The seat nearest to the door you enter is the best seat. Give this seat to the senior member of your party or to your client. Before entering the cab ahead of your client or boss, say, "Let me go ahead and slide in across the seat." If there are three passengers, the most junior member of your group will sit in the middle seat.

If your driver is smoking, you may ask him not to smoke. Or better yet, ask for another cab; I do. If the radio is loud, you certainly may ask that it be lowered or turned off. Before entering the cab, be sure that it has a working heater or an air conditioner. Definitely say something if you feel your driver is speeding, or if he or she is taking a longer or incorrect route (Tuckerman and Dunnan 1995). While traditionally the senior member of your group pays the fare, be prepared to pay the bill on behalf of your group. Obtain and save the receipt.

LIMOUSINE PROTOCOL

If you are a guest, and the hotel, company, or your host sends a limousine for you, the limousine is referred to as a *car*. Never refer to it as a *limo*. Since the car was hired for you, you are not required to tip the driver unless he or she not only drives but also carries all of your materials into the hotel or conference center or gives you a particularly excellent tour of the area as he or she drives. Limousine drivers have always been kind to me; I tip them between five and ten dollars depending on the length of the drive and extent of service.

If you are traveling with senior personnel, remember that the best seat in a limousine is the passenger seat closest to the curb. This is the passenger seat that is not behind the driver and where you will seat the senior person in your party.

Your host will generally get into the car first so that the guests do not have to slide over. Should you graciously have to take the seat next to the limousine driver, consider this an opportunity. Having befriended several limousine drivers this way, I now have a friendly and dependable network should I need any travel, city, or entertainment advice from insiders in a number of locations. No cell phone calls should be made or answered if other passengers are in the car with you.

DOORS

In the "Diversity" section of chapter 2, I talk about business being gender blind. This absolutely holds true in business when deciding who goes through a door first. You will always hold the door open for your guest. Period. You will always hold the door open for a senior executive. Other than that, in business, whoever gets to the door first is the one who opens it for his or her colleagues.

Having said that, let's get real. There is a difference between social and business etiquette. Traditional men who live by a gentleman's code will always hold the door open for a woman or an elder. These men would be unable to do otherwise. If you are a woman in business and a man opens a door for you, be appreciative. Go through the door and say thank you.

Allow people who are leaving a building or a room to exit through the door first before you attempt to enter the building or room. Please look behind you as you enter or exit a building to make sure that you are not shutting the door on someone entering or exiting right behind you.

I know that each of you, male or female, young or ageless, will always assist a colleague who is carrying a large stack of anything, regardless of title and position.

Revolving Doors

Whoever gets there first goes through first—if you are with your colleagues. Generally, let your senior executives go through first. But it gets a little tricky. If the door is already in motion, do let your guest or the senior executive go through first. If it is not, then you must do the heavy lifting. Go though first and wait on the other side to direct your guest or executive to his or her destination. You may first want to say, "Allow me to start the revolving door for you. I'll be on the other side to show you to the conference room."

ELEVATORS

Elevator etiquette is mostly common sense. Socially, of course, gentlemen always stay back to allow women and older citizens to enter and exit an elevator. Of course, gentlemen always take hats and caps off in an elevator.

Now let's look at this protocol on a busy, snowy, and generally stress inducing midtown New York City workday. In an elevator crowded with lots of people wearing heavy overcoats and holding umbrellas, totes, and briefcases, it's fine for men to keep their hats on. Actually, I don't know with which of your extra hands you had planned to remove your hat.

If you are in a crowded office building, don't stand on ceremony, just get in the elevator. Having entered an empty elevator, stand to the side near the door. No sense fighting your way out from the back of the elevator cab later. Since you are in first and nearest to the control panel, ask newcomers, "What floor?" Press the correct button for them. You will want to hold the *open* button when the doors open so that no one gets smashed while exiting. You may need to step out of the elevator to allow others in the back to exit. Then step back in. Again, remember that a big part of manners is common sense.

When other passengers are present, not only is it considered rude to use your cell phone in an elevator, but you may be sharing confidential work related or personal information with strangers.

STAIRS, ESCALATORS, AND MOVING WALKWAYS

Stairs, escalators, and moving walkways all have the same protocol. Always stand to the right. Never stand to the left or in the middle. That's it. Just move yourself over to the right and stay there. There are actually people behind you who may need to get somewhere in a hurry, and there you are in front, blocking the entire pathway. That's exactly like when you're in the grocery store and someone decides to leave a shopping cart right in the middle of the aisle, parked sideways. Don't be that shopping cart. Please try to make life a little easier for everyone else.

Socially, the man precedes the woman when going down an escalator. The woman precedes the man when going up an escalator. In business, just get on the escalator. If the CEO of your company or your supervisor is traveling with you, stand aside so that he or she may enter the escalator first.

Oh, and if you're at the airport on one of those moving walkways, please know that your luggage, placed like that shopping cart, may cause me to miss my plane. Think common sense. Think courtesy.

HOTELS

As a business traveler, you will find that your hotel has meeting rooms, computers, fax machines, copiers, wireless access to the Internet in your room, and a complete business center—everything you need. Speak with the hotel concierge to get advice on business amenities and to find out when your seminar or meeting begins.

This is a good time to observe what the competition does well. What can you learn? Back home, you'll want to let your general manager and your team know about creative services and innovative practices of the competition.

Be ready to compliment excellence. If this is not your brand, know that hotel associates are aware of your affiliation and will be watching your behavior. Be gracious and wonderful. This suggestion is also meant for airline, casino, restaurant, and other hospitality industry personnel who are visiting the competition.

Always check your brand's travel policies and save all business travel receipts. Now just dive into one of the hotel's plush robes and relax.

MOTELS

Your business travel may take you to a motel. Staying at a motel can be very advantageous for the business traveler. Most motel chains have located their properties near major highways, thoroughfares, and airports. Many motels do not have coffee shops, but they put out a really first-rate breakfast for their overnight guests. Most motels are strategically located within easy walking distance of a variety of traveler friendly restaurants.

This experience is more basic than a hotel stay. You get your own ice and carry your own bags to your room. Unlike a resort or a four or five star hotel, the room will not be luxurious. If you need extra towels, shampoo, or a wake-up call, just telephone the front desk.

There is usually a small gym and sometimes a pool and a hot tub on the property. You will either have wireless Internet access in your room or access to computers and the Internet in the motel's business center. Snacks and candy are available in vending machines, and most motels have complimentary hot coffee, tea, and cookies or fruit available in the front lobby.

BED-AND-BREAKFAST LODGING

Business and personal travel anywhere in the world may take you to a bed-and-breakfast (B and B), especially if you are unable to obtain a room at a large and overbooked hotel. This is often a very good thing. My experiences in Europe at bed-and-breakfasts have been wonderful.

You will be greeted by friendly people; most likely, the host (who may also be the owner) will show you to your room. Here is where I again say to pack light. I remember dragging a heavy suitcase up three flights of steep and creaky stairs at a lovely old B and B in Dublin. The experience left me with a temporary limp. Taking so much with me on that trip was a huge mistake.

On the plus side, the breakfasts are fairly amazing. Breakfast is included in the price of the room. Usually there is an unbelievable choice and amount of food. Simpler B and Bs may offer a continental breakfast of juice, coffee, bread, rolls, and jam.

You'll need to keep the following in mind when staying at a B and B:

- You may be sharing a bathroom, so get in and out as quickly as possible and leave the bathroom neat and clean.

- Your host probably lives in the B and B; never enter the host's living area.
- Remember that this is like a house; you need to be quiet in the halls and public areas at night so you don't awaken other exhausted guests (Mitchell 2004).
- While tipping is not required at a B and B, you may tip a housekeeper or other staff member who was particularly helpful during your stay.

You will find the rooms charming. You may also find the rooms to be extraordinarily cold. In older lodgings, the heating may have been around since the Napoleonic Wars. If you are traveling during the winter, take along very warm pajamas and lots of socks. Trust me on this.

THE PRIVATE HOME

Some clients and friends would not dream of having you stay anywhere except at their home. Or you may end up there because of weather conditions that cause your flight to be cancelled. While this arrangement would not be my first choice, if you find yourself as a houseguest, be gracious.

If this is a planned stay, you will arrive with a hostess gift. A hostess gift is mandatory, and the following should be considered before picking one out:

- Stay away from gifts of wine unless you know that your client is an avid collector and you have had a sommelier (a knowledgeable wine professional) assist you with the selection.
- You can always arrive with a box of very good chocolates, a gourmet selection of herbs and spices, a handsome serving tray, or monogrammed linen cocktail napkins.
- You may also want to send a gift of flowers after your visit. Some visitors send these prior to the visit.

If you are conducting business during the day, take this house visit out of the business context in the evening. Give your hosts as much space as possible. Take a walk or read a book in your room. Be sure to pack a robe that provides appropriate coverage should the bathroom you are assigned be in a hallway and not connected to your sleeping quarters.

Let your hosts know in advance that you are taking them out to dinner or to lunch. If invited to do so, join in on family or group activities, such as walks and games. It's very important that you remember to be kind to your hosts' children and pets. Also important is remembering electronic etiquette during your visit with the following rules:

- Remember that cell phones and other electronics are just as annoying in a private home as they are in public places.
- Ask permission before logging on to your host's computer or WiFi, and limit your time online.
- Never have either personal or business telephone calls forwarded to your hosts' home. Use your cell phone, which is, of course, set on vibrate (Mitchell 2004).

If your hosts have a staff, I know you will be cheerful and respectful. Tipping is discretionary in a private home and is based on extent of service. You may telephone or e-mail your hosts to let them know that you have arrived home, and you may thank them at that time. This electronic communication does not replace your thank-you letter. Since you are hardly ordinary, you will absolutely handwrite your thank-you letter or note right away.

HOSTING A GUEST ON PROPERTY

When your out-of-town business guest will be lodging at your facility, it is both efficient and thoughtful to create and send to your guest a one page information sheet that lists telephone numbers and company names of ground transportation from the airport (taxicab, limousine, car rental, or airport van) to your location. If the guest is renting a car, send or e-mail area maps.

Provide contact numbers for yourself and others at your property. Let your guest know if you will be picking him or her up at the airport, and exactly where at the airport you will be waiting. Provide your guest with information about your conference agenda, meal arrangements, and expected weather conditions well before the date of travel.

If you have not met your guest at the airport, be at your meeting early so that you can greet this out-of-towner, or arrange to meet for breakfast on the day of your meeting. Should the arrival be early enough, give your business guests a tour of your property, but remember that this may have been a very long day for them. Amenities like bottled water and fruit or sweets provided in the room will be well received, as will your personal welcome note.

TRADE SHOWS AND CONVENTIONS

Trade shows and conventions are great opportunities to cement valuable business relations and to acquire cutting edge industry knowledge. If you are the associate behind the vendor's booth, remember that your colleagues, potential clients, and guests are watching you. This is not the time to scratch an itch or sneak a peek into your mirror to see what may be caught between your teeth. Avoid eating and drinking in the booth during your shift.

Please do not chat with associates, read a magazine, speak on your cell phone, use your tablet, text, or interrupt other exhibitors. The public will perceive you as being bored and uninterested in your brand. Know everything there is to know about your brand and your property or company. Do more listening to your potential clients and guests than talking. Smile. Be approachable.

If you are attending a trade show or convention as a representative of your property, brand, or organization, make lots of new professional friends and enjoy the company of your colleagues. Your registration materials will guide you regarding the dress code and times of all sessions, meals, and other activities.

Arrive everywhere on time, dressed appropriately. Remember that you are being evaluated by your peers. Be alert for new ideas that you may be able to take back to your team.

TRAVELING WITH ASSOCIATES

Traveling with your associates can make the trip either perfectly wonderful or perfectly unpleasant. It's good when there are two or more of you to cover different conference sessions and exchange information and new knowledge. If it's a one or two day trip, there shouldn't be any difficulties.

Remember that no one said your colleagues have to become your best friends. You may find it difficult to be with your teammates all day at meetings, breakfast, lunch, and dinner, and in some cases have to share a hotel or motel room.

Should you want to sit with other people at meetings and seminars, do so. Make a breakfast appointment with a new business contact. If your associates have made dinner arrangements with colleagues, make arrangements with other colleagues or else just wash your hair, review your notes, and get to bed early (Fox 2001). This way everyone goes back to work rested, and you remain professional friends.

TRAVELING ALONE

I did say that business is gender blind. Well, I fibbed just a little bit in the area of traveling alone. Men and women travelers must each be prudent regarding where they stay, shop, dine, and sightsee in an unfamiliar city. Various business areas and neighborhoods will be unknown to you.

It can be a little easier for men to travel by themselves in terms of safety. Still, both men and women need to have a heart-to-heart with their concierge so that they are directed to not only excellent destinations but safe ones as well. Don't be afraid to ask. You will always be safer dining out or sightseeing in an unfamiliar city if you stay with your business group.

For the Woman Traveler

When you are not at your business or seminar site and a stranger attempts to speak with you, use common sense. If you feel uncomfortable, just do not answer. Step away from this person. For a woman traveler in a foreign country, this is doubly true when on a public street. Walk to the nearest populated place, a store, or a restaurant.

When traveling alone, if I am ahead of schedule, I may see a movie or attend a cultural event. I have learned to take an aisle seat at these events so that I am able to move away quickly if anyone next to me behaves inappropriately.

For Men and Women Travelers

Cashing a check where you are lodging is a convenient alternative to using an ATM. If your only choice is to use an ATM, remain alert when withdrawing money. An ATM is not any more secure just because it is located in a highly trafficked area. Here are some tips to make your withdrawal more safe:

- Use your body to shield the ATM keyboard from other people waiting behind you.
- Never count money at the machine.
- Quickly place the money in your pocket or handbag.
- This is not the time to dig to the bottom of your purse or briefcase looking for your sunglasses.

Now that you have cash, you may be debating whether to order room service or venture out into the property's dining room. Go for the dining room; you just may have a wonderful evening.

We all know that it's rude to read at the dinner table when you are with others. However, you may be more comfortable, when by yourself, in taking a book, tablet, e-reader, or newspaper with you to read while waiting for your meal to arrive. Know that there is another side to the book/newspaper route. If you are comfortable in your hotel's dining room and a stranded diner strikes up a conversation, you may wish to put your book down and reach out to another unaccompanied traveler. I have gained many an entertaining dining companion and business contact this way. I recommend inviting strangers to your table only within the protective confines of the property.

CHAPTER 7

Gratuities
Tipping for Service

The custom of tipping is thought to have originated in England in the 1700s or earlier. One story has it that pub owners left containers out so that thirsty travelers would leave a tip in the container as soon as they entered the establishment. Tip stands for "to insure promptness." (You may recognize that the spelling should actually be *ensure*, not *insure*.) Anyway, the server saw the coins dropped into the bucket or bowl and ran right over to take the patron's food or beverage order (Von Drachenfels 2000).

Another version is that English businessmen would give a shilling or two to a stagecoach driver "to insure promptness." They wanted their mail to be delivered promptly. This was insurance that the driver would stay on his route and not stop and sleep, drink, or visit lady friends. Using coachmen to deliver private mail instead of the government post boys, who carried mail by horseback, was considered an act of bribery and, as such, was illegal (Bayne-Powell 1972).

Still another story is that the lords of the manor would occasionally reward their servants with a coin, or the "tip" of gold or silver cut off from a larger coin. This act of "clipping" was made illegal in the 1600s, as it was thought to undermine the currency of England. Unscrupulous people would melt these pure gold and silver tips into bars, combining them with copper. They would then sell the bars to a goldsmith as pure (George 2014).

GENERAL GUIDELINES

Regardless of how it all started, tips are a bit different today. While there are general guidelines, the actual amount of the tip is up to the patron and shows his or her appreciation for level of service or lack thereof. Tips are correctly adjusted based on your own financial circumstances and on your locale.

Airports

At airports, if you are checking in at curbside, tip skycaps $1 to $2 per piece of luggage, more if the luggage is particularly heavy or bulky. If the skycap carries your luggage into the terminal, tip him or her at least $2 per bag.

Hotels

At your hotel, you will tip the doorman at least $1 to $2 per bag if he or she carries luggage inside for you. Tip the doorman $1 or $2 if he or she hails a taxi for you. You will tip $1 or $2 per bag when the bellman arrives at your room. Add an extra $2 to the tip if the bellman also brings ice or extra hangers or towels to your room. In larger cities, $2 per bag is customary.

Should the bellman deliver flowers or packages to your room, tip $1 to $2. Don't forget the parking valet who will retrieve your rental car; give the parking valet $2 to $3 or even more if it's a difficult retrieval because of rain, sleet, or snow.

Satisfied travelers leave the housekeeper $3 per night per person. You, of course, may leave more, up to $5 per night per person, depending on both the number of people attended to and the level of service. Leave this money in the room, in an envelope, on the last day of your stay. If you know your housekeeper's name, do write it on the front of the envelope. If not, simply write the word *housekeeping* on the front of the envelope.

You do not tip your concierge unless he or she snags some impossible to get tickets to an opening night or other in demand venue. This level of expertise calls for a tip of $20 per ticket. If the concierge gets you into a restaurant with a waiting list a mile long, tip $10. If you ask your concierge to pack and mail one or more packages for you, tip him or her between $10 and $20.

I like to give the head valet a $20 bill when I arrive at a high-end hotel. I suggest that you do the same. Because of your work or play, you will need local transportation. This person will always remember your thoughtfulness. The head valet can magically make a taxi appear when none seems to be available. Or you may be rewarded with the use of a house car (limousine) that will take you to meetings and restaurants at no additional charge. Should you be surprised with a house car, tip the driver $5 for short trips.

Motels

It is customary to leave the housekeeper $2 or $3 per night, per person. Leave this money each day on your pillow to ensure that the person cleaning your room that day receives the tip. If you have an envelope in which to leave the tip, write the word *housekeeping* on the front of the envelope.

Bed-and-Breakfast Lodging

Tipping is not required at a B and B. You may wish to tip a housekeeper or other staff member who was particularly helpful during your stay.

Private Homes

Tipping the staff is not required in a private home. However, if you feel that a staff member has gone above and beyond for you, you may do so very discreetly. Place the money in an envelope and find a private moment to thank the employee.

In homes or estates with full staffs (chef, housekeepers, driver, gardener, etc.), consult with the butler regarding how to show your monetary appreciation to the entire staff. The butler's gratuity is given to him separately, in a sealed envelope (Leutert 2013). The amount of the butler's tip is based on extent of service.

A handwritten letter of appreciation addressed to the entire staff is always appropriate. Compliment your hosts about the exemplary service.

Ships

Shipboard, you will give your steward $2 per each bag carried to your cabin. The ship will automatically add gratuities for everyone with whom you come into contact during your cruise. All the same, here are the realistic guidelines. Think about giving your cabin steward an additional $25 or more for immaculately cleaning your room and providing flawless nightly turndown service.

If you have a suite and a butler, he or she is tipped between $4 and $5 a day. This tip is given at the end of the cruise. If you have guests or a party in your suite and your reception involves setting up, serving, or cleaning up by your butler, take this into consideration. Add a minimum of $25 or even more to his or her tip.

The dining room staff remains with you throughout the cruise, and it is traditional to give $25 or more for a job well done. Tip the room service personnel $1 or $2 for room deliveries and at least $2 for each individual meal brought to your cabin. The 15 to 20 percent guideline applies to all personal services you receive on board: haircuts, manicures, massages, and any other spa services.

Trains

If you are traveling by rail and are in a sleeping car, tip the attendant about $3 per person. Tip more if the attendant has given you extra assistance or stellar service.

Taxicab

When traveling by taxi, tip the driver $1 per bag plus 15 to 20 percent on top of the fare. Of course, if the driver is difficult or rude, your tip will reflect this.

Limousines

If you have arranged for your own limousine, tip 20 percent of the bill. If the car was hired for you, you are not required to tip the driver. However, I always tip between $5 and $10 depending on the length of the drive.

Hotel Vans

If you take a hotel van from or to the airport, tip the driver $1 per bag. If the bag is larger or very heavy, tip more. I generally tip a minimum of $2 for the trip to or from the hotel.

Bus Travel

On commercial bus lines, the driver is never tipped. You do tip the driver and the tour guide if you are on a bus tour. Passengers often take up a collection for this purpose. The rate is $3 to $5 per day, per person, for the guide and $2 to $4 per day, per person, for the driver.

You do not have to tip with the group, and if you are especially satisfied with the tour, you may tip individually. It is considered polite to place either kind of tip in a sealed envelope. Some groups also place a note of thanks in the envelope.

Tow Trucks

If you've had your tire changed, your car jump started, or your car door unlocked, or if you have been driven to the repair shop with your car in tow, tip the service person $5. This holds true even if you are a member of an automobile club or have a prepaid car service arrangement with your dealership. Your car will most likely break down at five o'clock Friday afternoon during a thunderstorm, on the expressway. Be patient. Other people are also having breakdowns.

Handyman

Each time you have a repair or other small job, tip between $5 and $10.

Quick Service Counters

When you grab your morning jumbo double octane latte at a quick service counter, you may wish to leave change in the tip jar. This is a nice thing to do, especially if you have established a relationship with the counter people. Generally 25¢ or whatever change you receive is fine. However, tipping is in no way required just because there is a jar on the counter. Tips are meant to reward special service.

Buffets

At a buffet, the server takes beverage orders and sees that your plates are cleared each time you return to the buffet. Since you serve yourself at a buffet, leaving a tip of 10 percent of the bill is customary. Leave up to 15 percent should your server provide exemplary service to your party.

Restaurants

The standard tip in a restaurant is 15 percent or up to 20 percent of the bill for exemplary service. Tip 20 percent when dining in a more upscale restaurant. I generally tip 20 percent in all types of restaurants if the service is up to par. If you hold the table for a long time because you are chatting with your clients or friends, tack on an extra 10 or 15 percent to the bill. The server has easily lost this much money by not being able to turn the table over to new guests.

In some restaurants, gratuities are automatically added to the bill. This may happen if your party is of six or more. This addition to your bill is usually stated on the menu; the amount of the added tip is generally 18 percent. Always check to see if a tip has been added into your total, just in case it was not stated on the menu. For excellent service, you may add more to this tip. In any restaurant, if a mistake has been made on your bill, quietly bring it to the attention of your server.

Maître d'Hôtel

In a very upscale restaurant, you will have a captain and a waiter assisting you. Some restaurants also have a maître d'hôtel, also called the maître d'. This person will show you to your table. While a tip is not required for this service alone, it is appropriate to tip this person $10 to $20 every few times you dine at this fine restaurant.

If you are hosting a number of guests, you will give separate tips to the maître d'hôtel or headwaiter, whichever one is in charge of overseeing the success of your function. Tip about $1 to $2 per guest depending on the custom in your area.

If you are establishing a new relationship at an elegant restaurant, you will want to tip the maître d' $10 to $20 the first time he or she seats you. The maître d' is properly tipped after he or she has seated your party. For larger parties, and depending on the occasion and level of service you are expecting, the tip can be as high as $100. The maître d' will absolutely remember you after that.

Captain and Server

You will tip 15 to 20 percent of the bill (minus taxes and wine); this tip goes to the captain and the server. Some higher-end restaurants have a line on the bill for the amount you are leaving to each one. The captain receives 25 percent of the tip and the server receives 75 percent of the tip.

If you are hosting a dinner at a restaurant, there may already be a service charge (tip) on the bill. If not, add your tip to the total.

Wine Steward

A male wine steward is called a *sommelier,* and a female wine steward is called a *sommelière.* This person receives 15 to 20 percent of the cost of the wine. If he or she has simply taken your order for the wine and only poured the first glass, the tip left is 10 percent. If there is no wine steward, you add the cost of the wine into the tip that you leave to your server and/or captain.

You will want to increase the standard wine steward tip if your group orders several bottles of wine and/or if the sommelier has paid special attention to you and/or your group. There may be a line on your bill where you can fill in the wine steward's tip. It is customary to pay the sommelier in cash as you are exiting the restaurant.

Busser

Unless the busser assists you with the cleanup when your plate of spaghetti goes into your lap or carries your drinks from the bar to your table, he or she is not tipped. Should the busser provide these services, tip him or her $1 to $2.

Bars

Tipping in bars is done in one of two ways. If you are simply having a drink in a bar, tip between 15 and 20 percent of your bill. Never leave less than $1. Should the bartender offer to run a tab for you or insists that you sample a special drink, tip this bartender 20 percent. If you are in a restaurant bar while waiting for your table to become available, you may have your tab added to your dinner bill or simply pay for your drinks and go in to dinner. In this case, leave $1 or $2 per drink.

Private Clubs

If you are in a private club, it is because you are either a member or the guest of a member. It is considered an honor to be a guest in a private club. Cash is not used in a private club. The tip is included on the monthly statement of the member. Only members may sign restaurant and bar bills. You would never offer to pay for a meal or a cocktail, and you would never tip if you are in a private club and are not a member.

Food Deliveries

The standard tip for fast food deliveries is 10 percent of the bill. A generous tip is 15 percent. Sometimes there will be a delivery charge of $2 or more on your bill. This charge may go to the owner (who may own the delivery truck or car) or to the delivery person to cover the costs of his or her gasoline and automobile insurance. The delivery charge is not considered when calculating your tip. Never tip this person less than $2. If your elevator is broken and he or she has to climb up several flights, or if the weather is bad, seriously consider raising the tip to 15 percent or more of the bill.

Washroom Attendant

Your attendant may hand you a towel (cloth or paper); the standard tip for this service is between 50¢ and $1. If the attendant is helpful in sewing on a hanging button, letting you know you need hair spray (and providing it), or getting the lint off your sports jacket, leave $2 or $3. It is customary to place this tip in a plate that is found near the sinks.

Coatroom Attendant

The standard tip for checking a coat or a raincoat is $1. Add a little more to this if you are also checking an umbrella, tote bag, or briefcase.

Parking Valet

The standard valet parking tip is $2. The tip is given when the valet brings your car to you. In difficult circumstances (sleet, hail, snow), the tip is $3 or more. In smaller cities, the tip is $1 or $2, and in larger cities, the tip may vary from $2 to $5.

Car Wash Attendant

Generally, there is a tip jar in which you will place $1 to $2. This tip is shared by the car washers and detailers. If your car has had any kind of detailing or waxing, tip between 10 and 15 percent of the bill.

Musician

If you and your companion request a special song, tip musicians $1 or $2. If a large party makes one or more requests, tip $5. If you occupy musicians throughout the evening, consider a tip of $10 or more.

Casinos

Keep in mind that tipping etiquette at casinos usually applies only when you are winning. As with all things etiquette, remember your manners. Friends, family, and perhaps even your employer may be watching. The following guidelines apply:

- *Blackjack*: Leave for the dealer a $5 chip per session. A session is the length of time a dealer works the table before a new dealer takes over. Sophisticated players may place a side bet of up to 10 percent of the winnings for the dealer.
- *Craps*: Leave for the dealer a $5 chip per session.
- *Keno*: The runners and writers are tipped at least $1 for the first ticket. If you win, add an additional 5 percent.
- *Poker*: Leave for the dealer at least a $5 chip per session. Classy players may want to add 10 percent of their winnings, not to exceed $25. Use common sense. Don't leave a $5 chip for your dealer if you are at the dollar poker table. A $1 tip is fine. On the other hand, if you find yourself the winner of a huge pot, the tip will be much more than just one $5 chip.
- *Roulette*: Tip at least one $5 chip per each session.
- *Slot machines*: Some casinos have a person called a *changer* for their slot machines. This person will give you whatever change you need while you are sitting at a slot machine. This person will also cash out your jackpot. Tip at least $1 per change made and 5 percent if you hit a jackpot. This jackpot tip should not exceed $25. Should your machine require a repair, tip this attendant at least $1.
- *Waiter/Waitress* (also called *server*): Please remember to tip your server at least a $1 chip for each free drink (PokerSource 2013).

Tipping etiquette varies by country. In New Zealand, Australia, and the United Kingdom, tipping is forbidden in casinos. When traveling out of your own country, speak with your hotel concierge to learn that country's casino tipping guidelines.

Personal Services

The general rule for all personal services (hairstylist, barber, waxing technician, massage therapist, nail technician) is to add a tip of 15 to 20 percent to the bill. The stylist's assistant who washes your hair will be tipped $2 or $3. In larger cities, he or she may be tipped $5 or more. If the assistant is also involved in applying, checking on, and washing out your color or bleach, tip him or her $5 to $10. If there is a separate colorist, he or she is tipped between $5 and $10 depending on the extent of the service. Use common sense when applying these general standards.

International Travel

If you are traveling internationally, speak with your travel agent or research your host country's tipping traditions online before your trip. Your international hotel's concierge will gladly fax or e-mail tipping guidelines to you.

HOLIDAY TIPPING/PERSONAL GUIDELINES

Holiday tipping can be confusing, so remember that these are only guidelines. Always consider your budget and the circumstances of the relationship. If you are going through a rough spot, consider baking a pie, cake, or cookies to show your appreciation. A card with a note of thanks is always appreciated. The holidays are a good time to write a letter of appreciation and send it to that person's employer.

Gifts can be in the form of cash, check, or gift card, each placed in a holiday card or an envelope with a note of appreciation. Your gift need not be monetary. It can be a special purchase that you know will be appreciated by the recipient.

Personal Assistant

Should you be fortunate to have a personal assistant in your home, this person is generally given one week's salary if they have worked with you for under a year. If the employment has been for a year or more, and if your circumstances allow it, give up to two weeks' salary.

Nanny

Nannies are generally given one week's salary if they have worked with you for under a year. If they've been with you longer, and if your circumstances allow it, give up to two weeks' salary.

Housekeeper

Housekeepers are generally given one week's salary if they have worked with you for under a year. If your housekeeper has been with you longer, and if your circumstances allow it, give up to two weeks' salary. If this person lives in your home, the gift may be as much as one month's salary along with a present.

Babysitter

The babysitter will either receive what you pay for two sittings or a small gift together with what you pay for one sitting. This suggestion is for your regular babysitter, not for someone who has sat for you only a couple of times during the year.

Personal Trainer

The suggested gift is the cost of one session but never less than $50.

Day Care Provider

Give anywhere from $25 up to $50 or even more according to the custom in your area. While the gift of cash is always appreciated, depending on your personal circumstances, some day care providers are given a lovely holiday gift.

Your Child's Teacher

Never give cash to this educational professional. A small gift will be appreciated.

Pet Groomer

Give this person the cost of one grooming session. You may want to combine this tip with a small gift.

Dog Walker

Give your dog walker the cost of one walking service.

Pool Cleaner

Tip your pool cleaner the equivalent of one cleaning service. If more than one person cleans the pool, this tip may be for both of them. Hand the tip to one cleaner and say, "Thank you both and have a happy holiday."

Massage Therapist

If you visit your massage therapist (or he or she visits you) on a regular basis, tip the equivalent of one session and a small gift for this very personal service. The term *masseuse* is used for a female massage therapist, and *masseur* is used for a male massage therapist.

Letter Carrier

In the United States, mail carriers may accept gifts of up to $20 in value. Different countries have different guidelines.

Gardener

It is appropriate to tip the gardener or yard worker between $20 and $50. If there is a crew of two or three workers, tip on the high side, and let the head gardener know that the tip is for all of them by saying, "Thank you both [or all three of you] and have a nice holiday."

Newspaper Deliverer

Give your newspaper deliverer between $10 and $35 depending on the custom in your area.

Doorman

In a residential building, give your doorman (or doormen) between $20 and $80 each. Your doorman may feed your goldfish, water plants, and hold your mail while you are on vacation. The services provided for you are invaluable. If one doorman is more essential to your well-being than the others, you may wish to supplement the tip with a small gift of appreciation that is given privately.

Elevator Operator

In a residential building, the elevator operator can easily become the most important person in your busy day. Besides the obvious job description, he or she may also perform services similar to those of your doorman, such as assisting with heavy packages or overseeing deliveries to your apartment. Give your well-loved elevator operator between $20 and $80 for the holidays.

Superintendent

The superintendent of a large building is generally not tipped during the year unless, from time to time, he or she provides some specific and special services for you. So at the holidays, take this into consideration. The suggested holiday tip will run from $20 to $80. If the supervisor does not live in the building and you rarely see him or her, $20 is appropriate.

Handyman

A handyman's holiday tip is optional. Throughout the year, each time you had a repair or other small job, you have been tipping between $5 and $10. Should you decide on a holiday tip, never tip less than $15. Depending on the amount of work completed and time devoted to your household repairs, the high end is $50.

Trash Collector

Tip each collector between $10 and $20.

Hairstylist or Barber

Holiday tipping can vary widely depending on the size of the city. A general rule is to tip the cost of one haircut, or at least $40. If your hairdresser or barber has become your friend and coconspirator in life, you may wish to add an appropriate present with the tip.

You may have a separate colorist or person who shampoos your hair. Give the staff at the beauty salon between $10 and $50 each (or a small gift) depending on what they have actually done for you throughout the year.

Nail Technician

Tip at least the cost of one manicure. In larger cities, the holiday tip will vary between $25 and $75. As this relationship is special, you may wish to add a gift along with the tip.

Waxing Technician

This too, is a very special relationship, and as with your nail technician, rates at least the cost of one waxing service up to about $25. A small gift along with the tip is also appropriate depending on the relationship.

Holiday Tipping When Traveling

When you are traveling for business or pleasure, tipping extra for Christmas or other holidays is not necessary and is not expected. You may certainly add an additional amount for the holiday if you wish.

Tipping on Your Own Property

Never tip your property's (or organization's) staff at any time during the year. For special efforts made throughout the year, a small and appropriate holiday gift, such as a book, home baked cookies, or a decorative item to place on a desk, will always be appreciated by any fellow employee with whom you have a special relationship.

CHAPTER 8

Your Professional Correspondence
Building Better Relationships—
Handwritten and E-mailed

You may be thinking, "My generation uses e-mail and texting. Why would I handwrite a thank-you note or a letter?" Sending a thank-you note or other personalized message by e-mail or text can make you seem very ordinary. The recipient reads it, presses the delete key, and *voilà*, the impression of you as being special is gone!

Make the effort to send a handwritten note to clients. Generally, the recipient places the note on his or her desk for a while and then places it in a file. Every time the recipient touches the note, he or she will smile and think, "Very nice. This person is considerate and has class."

However, business etiquette does evolve. Technology professionals are one exception to the handwritten note rule. Technology associates may correctly respond to other technology professionals with an e-mailed thank-you note. If this is an interview meal for a technical position, then an electronic thank-you is also appropriate for technology associates. Those of you who are not technology professionals but who communicate with colleagues worldwide by telephone, e-mail, or social networking may also appropriately e-mail your thank-you for a gift or other kindness.

Think carefully and appropriately as you craft your note, because your message will help to build a better business or personal relationship. These stronger relationships will lead to surprising opportunities, because you are known and remembered.

THANK-YOU NOTES

You may be thanking someone for a gift. You may want to show appreciation to guests, vendors, a speaker, or someone who has sent you a wonderful business referral. Most important is letting associates and others know that their work is appreciated. When one of your associates receives a thank-you note from you, it will have special meaning and importance. This note costs almost nothing, and yet it is actually priceless.

So now you're saying, "I'm not a good writer." The rules are embarrassingly simple. Check for spelling and grammatical errors and keep your correspondence short. Think courtesy and clarity. Get to the point and exit! Bad handwriting? If your writing really can't be read, go ahead and type a nice thank-you note. The note will go something like this:

> *Dear George,*
> *Thank you so much for being our guest speaker at the hotel's quarterly pep rally. The associates were energized by your message.*
> *Thank you again; your speech was just wonderful!*
> *Warm wishes,*
> *Annie Animated*

CONDOLENCE LETTERS

The purpose of a condolence letter is to comfort others. Sooner or later, you will probably need to write a condolence letter to one of your colleagues or to the family of a colleague. An example is:

> *Dear Helen,*
> *Please accept my deepest sympathy for your loss. Robert was such an important part of our team. He was always cheerful and willing to help others. Please let me know if any one of us at the airline can be of assistance during this trying time.*
> *Sincerely,*
> *Susan Sympathy*

If you wish to send a purchased sympathy card instead of writing a letter, be sure to add a personal note, such as:

> *Dear Helen,*
> *We are thinking about you during this difficult time.*
> *Sincerely,*
> *Connie and Cole Concerned*

If you are unsure of the deceased's religion, it's best to send a card that is religiously neutral.

You and/or the team may wish to make a charitable donation to honor the deceased. If you do this, let the family know by writing something like this on the condolence card (or in your letter):

> *Dear Mr. and Mrs. Jones,*
> *To honor Lilly's work with animals, we've made a donation in her memory to the Humane Society of the United States.*
> *Sincerely,*
> *The Culinary Team*

Check your organization's policy regarding sending flowers and making donations if you are doing so on behalf of the organization itself.

Your colleagues may have occasion to mourn a beloved pet. Sadness is sadness and loss is loss. This pet was a family member, and your coworker will be having a difficult time. Yes, write your friend a condolence note or send a card and write a heartfelt message on it. Everyone handles mourning in his or her own way, whether we find ourselves missing a person or a pet.

COWORKER ILLNESS

Remember to send a card or a letter to coworkers who are ill. Your team members are also your friends. It can be very lonely recovering in isolation. Consider carefully before sending an e-mail or a text. Your ill coworker may not be up to answering it. Here is an example:

> Dear Bernice,
> I hope you are well on your way to recovery. You and your home baked cookies are missed!
> Warmest wishes,
> Front Desk Fanny

Follow up the note with a personal telephone call. Knowing that your team is thinking about you can be a positive motivation to get well and return to work.

Should your coworker be diagnosed with a terminal illness, it is very understandable if you are uncomfortable and don't know what to do or say. Please give your friend the same kind support that he or she has always received from you. Visit and listen. Bring something that you know is liked. This can be a favorite food, home baked cookies, or cheerful yellow daisies. Your kindness will be appreciated, and as with all things in business or social etiquette, it is the right thing to do.

CONGRATULATORY LETTERS

These are certainly easy letters to write. They're cheerful and upbeat. You may want to write congratulatory letters to your coworkers for promotions, completing college, receiving an award, a personal accomplishment, coming to the team's rescue, and any of a countless number of happy events. Remember that these types of letters may be kept for years by the ecstatic recipient. Your letter might read:

> *Dear Ferdinand,*
> *Congratulations on having your delightful children's story published. This is such a wonderful accomplishment! Again, sincere congratulations.*
> *Warmly,*
> *Gushing Gussie*

BUSINESS LETTERS

No matter the type of business letter you are writing, it is essential that you use good quality letterhead and a first class printer. You may be writing to a guest, a vendor, or your corporate headquarters. You can have a trusted associate review your letter. I recommend purchasing a stylebook, such as *The Elements of Style: Fourth Edition* (Strunk and White 2000). These books can be purchased online or at most bookstores, and they will show you how to write concise and easily understood letters for any occasion.

So, plan your letter. Decide what is essential and present your points in an order that makes sense. Check not only for content but for tone, grammar, spelling, and punctuation. Now edit it; it's probably too long, and you don't want to lose your reader's attention. Edit it again and remember that if you are not on a first-name basis with the recipient, you should end the letter with "Very truly yours" or "Sincerely." It is only when you are on a first-name basis with the addressee that you may correctly end your business letter with, "Kind regards," "Best wishes," or "All the best."

MEMORANDA

The only thing I remember about my high school senior English class is learning the difference between *memoranda* and *memorandum.* Memorandum means one; memoranda is the plural. Let's just call them *memos.* Memos are generally used to make an announcement or to publicize employee information, like news about an added health insurance benefit or a change in the date of the annual picnic.

A memo is often posted in a work area where it is reasonable that all employees can read it. I mention this because you never want to write a memo that is critical, confidential, or not meant for the public to see. Memos are also posted online, on in-house company intranets.

LETTERS OF APOLOGY

Yes, after apologizing in person to someone you have offended, a follow-up letter is the mannerly thing to do. That letter will go like this:

> *Dear Mrs. General Manager's Wife,*
> *Please accept my sincere apology for having spilled red wine on your lovely white tablecloth.*
> *I have asked my dry cleaner to call you to arrange a pickup time so that the cloth can be professionally cleaned. I hope that you will forgive my clumsiness.*
> *Sincerely,*
> *Hopeless Hanna*

WELCOME NOTES

Welcome notes are guaranteed to make your guests smile, especially when accompanied by strawberries and chocolates. These are the happiest notes to write.

> *Dear Dr. and Mrs. Impressive Couple,*
> *Welcome to the Sunny Shores Hotel. We are so happy to have you as our guests. My extension is 1111. Please let me know how I may assist you in enjoying your stay.*

Very truly yours,
Ethel Enthusiastic
Front Desk Associate

Don't forget to write your title after you sign your name. Your guests need to know exactly who you are.

Another type of welcome note is the one you send to an associate who is new to your property or organization. Do you remember your first day at work? You really didn't know anyone. Why not write a welcome note to new associates? This small act will make each new associate feel wonderful. Always try to make people feel wonderful. Your mantra is kindness. Yes, it can be a purchased card signed by the entire team. The point is that it's the right thing to do. Little gestures go a long way.

STAYING CONNECTED NOTES

Don't wait until you need something from an individual to remember that person. Stay in touch with your vendors, clients, business associates, and guests throughout the year. You can mail birthday, congratulatory, and holiday cards. Whenever I see a newspaper or magazine article that would interest a past client or valued vendor, I clip it and send it along with a nice, short note. More often than not, I am rewarded with a telephone call thanking me for staying in touch.

Writing that touches the reader will build better relationships. These stronger relationships will lead to surprising opportunities because you are known and remembered as special.

RESPONDING TO INVITATIONS

Your professional life in hospitality management guarantees that at some point in your career, you will be invited to various engagements. Answer invitations within one week of receipt. Your invitation may have these letters written on it: RSVP. This is shorthand for the French phrase *Répondez s'il vous plaît*, or "please respond." RSVP may also be written as R.S.V.P. or R.s.v.p. Other possibilities are "Please reply," "Please respond," or "The favour of a reply is requested." On a formal invitation, *favour* is spelled the British way, instead of the American *favor*. If the invitation requests the "honour" of your presence, then again the word will be spelled in the British, not the American ("honor"), manner.

Your invitation may have a reply card enclosed. The reply card will already have a stamp on it and a mailing address. Fill out the reply card. There will be a space for your name and an area to fill in that lets the host know you are attending. If you are not attending, write the word *not* in this area. There will be the letter *M* written on the reply card. Next to the *M*, fill in *Mr.*, *Ms.*, *Miss*, or *Mrs.* as appropriate. A person with a title—such as Father, Sister, or Dr.— crosses out the *M* and writes the appropriate title. Other times, the words *accepts* or *regrets* are on the reply card with a space next to each. Check off the appropriate response by the right word.

> *The favour of a reply is requested*
> *M__Will__attend*
> *Sunday, August twenty-third*

Sometimes the invitation will not have a reply card but will ask that you telephone or e-mail to confirm your attendance. Other invitations will ask for "regrets only." This means that you respond only if you are unable to attend. It's very important to respond, as your host has worked hard to make sure that there is enough food and seating for all guests. Again, remember to answer your invitation within one week of receipt.

Very formal invitations are entirely different. Whether accepting or not, there is no fill-in-the-blank reply card enclosed with the invitation. Instead, you reply on a plain and conservative notepaper. The reply is handwritten. You follow the exact format of the invitation itself:

> *Ms. Fiona Formal accepts with pleasure*
> *Mr. and Mrs. Best Client's kind invitation to dinner*

on Saturday, November the twentieth
at half after seven o'clock

The invitation may advise, on the lower right hand corner, whether the party is "Black tie" or "Black tie optional." Or it may say, "Cocktail attire." In chapter 11, "The Power of Your Wardrobe," I will talk about how you, the savvy professional, will dress for both work and social occasions.

Invitations are addressed only to the persons who are actually invited to the event. Unless the invitation specifically says, "Mr. Conrad Concierge and Guest," or in the case of a formal invitation, "Ms. Constance Concierge and Escort," never bring anyone else with you to a party. Of course you would never bring children with you to a reception of any kind unless the children have been specifically invited.

EXTENDING INVITATIONS

You may be in charge of extending invitations for a property sponsored affair. There are formal and informal invitations. In the "Responding to Invitations" section of this chapter, I discussed reply cards. Reply cards are always mailed with formal invitations. Make sure your reply cards are sent out to guests with both a return address and a stamp on them.

Traditionally, formal invitations are engraved on white or ecru (this comes from a French word meaning unbleached or raw; the color is a pale grey-yellow or a pale yellow-brown) stock with black ink. The print (also called the *font*) is generally English Script, Shaded Roman, Times Roman, Palatino, or Shaded Antique Roman. Informal invitations also can have reply cards, or the informal invitation may ask for the RSVP by telephone or by e-mail.

Informal invitations may be extended on brand letterhead in your own, your general manager's, or another appropriate team member's personal handwriting. Your marketing department may create imaginative invitations for the event. Stationery stores are a wonderful and helpful resource.

Informal invitations can also be purchased. If you do this, be sure to write a personal message on each, such as, "Looking forward to seeing you." If the invitation is only for cocktails or tea, make sure this is included as part of the written message:

The Marketing Team Invites you
to cocktails for the benefit of
The Orphan's Relief Fund on Thursday, October 13th 6–8 o'clock
The Magnificent Manor Hotel 2101 Park Avenue
RSVP (797) 823-1951 Business attire

If you are in a large city and your facility is well known, it is not necessary to place the city name on any invitation. If you do use the city name, never include a zip code on the face of the invitation.

Outside of work, if you are arranging a wedding, birthday, or other party, never print on the invitation "No gifts, please." Never include a note that money is preferable to a gift. It is your guest's pleasure to purchase a gift for you. More to the point, it is not up to the host to have been expecting a gift in the first place.

E-VITES—ELECTRONIC INVITATIONS

E-vites, or electronic invitations, are invitations that are extended via e-mail to large numbers of people. E-vites are used by very fine corporations, charities, and marketing firms as reminders about upcoming functions. They are often sent as a follow-up to the mailed invitation. Consider using e-vites as "hold the date" notifications for upcoming business events, such as special guest promotions, and for upcoming personal events, such as weddings. E-vites are used by hotels, airlines, and restaurants to advertise special rates and promotions. Use E-vites to invite professional society members to meetings and other events. E-vites are also used for children's birthday parties.

If used as the invitation itself, an e-vite is extremely informal. When a mass e-vite is sent by an individual, inviting guests to share some important personal milestone, it is possible for clients, friends, or family to feel that the time was not made to extend a sincere and meaningful invitation. Consider purchasing packets of preprinted, festive invitations that are inexpensive and found in party shops and at drugstores. If your get-together is small, call personally and invite your guests.

USING YOUR STATIONERY WARDROBE

Communicating is the most important thing that you do all day, every day. Your brand will provide the appropriate letterhead and other stationery needed to support your professional correspondence. Once you have the right tools to do the job, please practice your written communication skills. You represent your exceptional brand. Do so with elegance and pride.

Your correspondence does not have to be long. In addition to seeing that your letters, notes, and memos get to the point and are grammatically correct, add a little bit of your personality to the mix. See if you can make the reader smile.

Never write a letter when you are angry or in the mood to complain. Sleep on it and regroup in the morning.

Corporate Letterhead

Your property will have 8½-by-11-inch letterhead that may have your brand's logo engraved on it along with the name of your organization and its address, telephone and fax numbers, business e-mail, and Website address. This letterhead is the stationery you will use for all of your property related business correspondence. There will also be plain, but matching, 8½-by-11-inch sheets that you may use as a second or third page if needed. You never use your letterhead for other than a first sheet.

Your brand will also supply matching business envelopes that are preprinted with your organization's name and address.

The Color of Your Ink

Traditionally, black or dark grey ink was always used for signing both official and personal correspondence. Today, there are very real concerns about signature authenticity on business documents. To ensure that you have an original signature on a document, it is recommended that you always use blue ink to sign official business correspondence and other related documents. Black ink is recommended for all other correspondence.

Correspondence Cards

Use correspondence cards when writing thank-you and other short notes. Your brand may supply correspondence cards on which you will write notes of greeting to your guests. You may use both sides of the card, placing the date on the bottom left of the card (*Wednesday, 26th*) and your closing (*Sincerely, Nancy New Associate*) to the bottom right. It is also thoughtful to write your title so that your guest understands what you do.

Correspondence cards are generally 4¼ by 6½ inches but can be a little larger. A white correspondence card with a beveled border or one that has a conservatively colored border is considered businesslike. My cards have a dark blue border. I use traditional black ink. Your brand may have specific corporate colors that it uses. Matching envelopes that are preprinted with your organization's name and address will be supplied along with the correspondence cards.

Informals

You may be given what are called *informals*. These are correspondence cards that fold over. The logo and company brand are found on the front; write your short note on the inside of the card. Matching envelopes that are preprinted with your organization's name and address will be supplied along with the informals.

Business Cards

These cards are about 3½ by 2 inches but can vary a little in size. Your card will have your company logo on it, the name of your brand, your name, your title, and all information needed to contact you: address, office telephone and cell numbers, street address, e-mail address, fax number, and the company's Website address.

Earlier, I stated that business cards should be immaculately clean, with all information up-to-date. Your card doesn't just represent you—it's also a proud representation of your brand. Never present a soiled, written on, or dog-eared card.

Personal Stationery

I'll bet you have nice shoes and appropriate suits or uniforms. Why not put the same thought into your personal stationery? When not at work, you will need to write various personal letters, requests, complaints, and letters of appreciation; thank-you letters for attending baby showers, luncheons, and christenings; letters in which you make a charitable donation; letters of thanks for being invited to interview for a possible promotion; and more. I suggest that you invest in a couple of boxes of white or cream colored 100 percent cotton fiber stationery and envelopes. In time, you may consider personalizing your stationery.

Personalizing is done by engraving (the print looks raised and three-dimensional), thermography (the print looks raised), or plain printing. Engraving is the most perfect looking and most expensive choice. Thermography is an outstanding and less expensive option. Plain printing is just that—plain.

Even if engraving or thermography are not in your budget at this time, it is always appropriate to use good quality white or cream colored 100 percent cotton fiber stationery for all of your personal correspondence. White is the color of choice for business correspondence. For thank-you notes and extending and replying to informal invitations, it's a good idea to have a box of classic ecru or white correspondence cards at home; you can never go wrong. Always use a black or very dark blue ink.

E-MAIL FOR THE HOLIDAYS

The classy thing to do is to send a holiday card instead of an e-mail greeting to your guests, clients, friends, relatives, and vendors. Having said that, it's a big and interconnected world, and your relationship with online global business colleagues and social media friends is a very big exception. It makes sense to send out holiday and other important regards by e-mail to these electronic friends and associates. Other ongoing business relationships may deserve a holiday card with a brief note and your signature. Consider this carefully.

Information technology professionals have always communicated by e-mail, so of course holiday greetings are no exception. If your business relationship is primarily through national or international telephone calls, Skype, FaceTime, or other web conferencing tools, sending your holiday greetings by e-mail makes sense.

When purchasing paper holiday cards, take your financial situation into consideration, and then look at the closeness of the relationship. Decide who will receive holiday greetings by e-mail. Generally, your guests, family, and closest friends will receive holiday cards.

Should you receive a card from either your rarely seen insurance agent or someone with whom you have no meaningful relationship, you do not have to reciprocate with a holiday card. Thank the person when you see him or her. A brief telephone call or an e-mail is also acceptable. Given our economic times, you may want to trim your personal holiday card list by telephoning or e-mailing local relatives and friends. Consider using your postage stamps for out-of-town friends and relatives.

Keep in mind that the holidays are the perfect time to do something special for your friends and professional associates. A holiday card or a handwritten note is always well received.

HOLIDAY CARDS

The holidays are a wonderful time to get back in touch with friends, guests, and acquaintances. Don't do this by simply signing your name to an array of cards that have some preprinted sentiment on them. This may come across as insincere. You are sincere, so write something on the card. It can be "Happy Holidays," "Merry Christmas," "Thinking of you at the holidays," "Let's get together in the New Year," or "All of the best, Long Lost Linda."

Send Chanukah cards to your Jewish friends. If you send a Jewish colleague a "Season's Greetings" card, it is very thoughtful to handwrite "Happy Chanukah" on the card. Send "Happy New Year" and "Season's Greetings" cards to your Muslim and Buddhist friends. If it's a mixed household of any kind, send a "Season's Greetings" card. Always use a black or very dark blue ink.

ANNUAL HOLIDAY LETTERS/E-MAILS

I'm not a fan of holiday letters. This is like sending out spam in longhand to lots of people you haven't kept up-to-date about your life's major events. There must be a reason you haven't updated them throughout the year. Still, a short one page holiday letter or e-mail, well composed and written in a happy tone, can be a delight to receive.

CHAPTER 9

Hosting Guests Who Have Disabilities
Are You Prepared?

There are millions of people worldwide who have disabilities. They are shopping, traveling, dining out, and applying for jobs. Think of the global spending power. Are you prepared to receive these guests?

Learn to offer a warm and appropriate business welcome. Be professionally ready to receive this large and important segment of your guest population. These are guidelines that you will use successfully throughout your career.

WELCOMING ETIQUETTE

You may have to ask your guest if he or she would like to shake hands. Use your judgment. People with limited hand use or who wear an artificial limb can usually shake hands. Shaking hands with the left hand is acceptable. A smile and a warm greeting are always correct. Speak directly to your guest, not to the person accompanying him or her.

Review accessibility prior to the visit. Restrooms, computers, and drinking fountains should be accessible. Review alternatives, such as a bottle of water and a drinking glass waiting on your desk.

When planning a company event, review possible barriers. If a barrier cannot be avoided, let your guest know this well ahead of time. Consider weather conditions if you are escorting your guest around your property or are receiving your guest outdoors. Allow more time for this meeting than you would generally. Be patient with both your guest and yourself.

GENERAL CONVERSATION ETIQUETTE

Even if your guest has brought an assistant, speak directly to your guest, never to the assistant or interpreter. Use your normal tone of voice. Never pretend to understand. Ask the person to repeat a phrase. Use written notes when necessary; your guest will appreciate the clarity. Offer a pen and pad.

Remember that anyone can make a mistake. Just relax. Offer an apology if you forget some courtesy.

GUESTS USING WHEELCHAIRS

When talking to a guest in a wheelchair, try to put yourself at eye level with the person; sit or kneel in front of him or her. Rearrange your office furniture as necessary to accommodate the wheelchair prior to your guest's arrival. If this is not possible, find a more suitable meeting place.

The wheelchair is personal space; never touch the chair unless the client or guest asks for your assistance. You might start the conversation by letting the guest know where accessible water fountains, telephones, computers, restrooms, charging stations for electronics, and other needed amenities are located (The Memphis Center for Independent Living 2014).

If your guest places a walker in your office, never attempt to be helpful by moving the walker to a more convenient location. This location may not be convenient for your guest. Leave the walker where it was placed by your guest. If the placement presents a danger to others, ask for your guest's permission prior to moving the walker.

SERVICE ANIMAL ETIQUETTE

According to the US Americans with Disabilities Act (ADA), a service animal performs some of the day-to-day functions and tasks that an individual with a disability cannot perform for himself or herself. The animal does not have to be licensed or certified by state or local government to meet this standard.

Under US federal law, you must admit a service animal to your property, regardless of health department or other state or local regulations. Your brand is not permitted to charge a deposit for allowing a service animal on property. You may charge a fee if the animal causes property damages only if this is the brand's regular practice with the animals of nondisabled guests.

Do not touch or feed a service animal. Do not make noise at the animal or attempt to distract it or the person it assists.

Be aware that not only dogs, but also monkeys and even small horses (and other animals) can be trained as official service animals. Some service animals will be wearing a vest, collar, or harness that alerts you to the fact that it is a working animal. Not all service animals wear this vest or harness (US Department of Justice 2013).

A DISABILITY THAT AFFECTS BRAIN FUNCTION

Take your time. Allow the person to show or tell you what he or she wants. Rephrase comments or questions for clarity. Focus directly on the client or guest when he or she responds to you (The Memphis Center for Independent Living 2014).

A DISABILITY THAT AFFECTS SPEECH

Have patience. This person may need extra time to complete a word or a thought on his or her own. Never pretend to understand. Ask for a phrase to be repeated; offer a pen and pad. Your guest may bring in an alphabet board or a computer that will synthesize speech. Know this prior to your meeting so that space for the device can be arranged. Never attempt to complete a thought, sentence, or word for your guest (US Department of Labor 2013).

A DISABILITY THAT AFFECTS VISION

Identify yourself, and identify everyone else present. Allow your client or guest to take your arm if he or she wishes. Walk slightly ahead. Mention doors, stairs, curbs, etc. as you approach them. Describe the layout of rooms. Be specific regarding locations of objects and furniture. Never move or rearrange objects or furniture during the visit. Never leave your client or guest without excusing yourself. Say where you are going and when you will return (US Department of Labor 2013).

HEARING IMPAIRED ETIQUETTE

Your client or guest will establish the communication mode: sign language, lip reading, or written notes. Even if your guest has brought a sign language interpreter, speak directly to your guest, never to the interpreter. Your lip reading client or guest will appreciate your facing him or her directly and speaking at a moderate pace.

Remember to stand directly in front of the light source (a window or a table lamp are examples) and to keep hands, pens, and food away from your face, as your guest may be lip reading. Use your normal tone of voice. Try simplifying and shortening sentences. Appropriate facial expressions are helpful (The Memphis Center for Independent Living 2014). Be patient with yourself.

CHAPTER 10

Special Guest Situations
You Set the Tone

Danny Meyer, president of the Union Square Hospitality Group, is known as America's most innovative restaurateur. He, his team, and his restaurants have earned an unheard of twenty-one James Beard Awards, the highest food and beverage honor possible in North America. In his book *Setting the Table,* Mr. Meyer writes clearly and gracefully about food, life, and what he describes as "a charitable mindset" in the hospitality arena. This view calls for each of us to assume the very best in ourselves, our coworkers, vendors, and guests (Meyer 2006). Mr. Meyer has been successful not only because of his excellent business sense, fine restaurants, and exceptional food, but because he adds the secret ingredients of optimism and kindness to the hospitality management menu.

Your guests may be savvy professionals, well-mannered travelers, or tired tourists. No matter. What's most important is that your guests, leaders, and team members see you as warm and professional. You must be able to respond to a variety of guest situations without hesitation. I know that you will display confidence, knowledge, and kindness.

GUEST MEETINGS ON PROPERTY

Never keep a client, vendor, or guest of any kind waiting longer than five minutes. If you are held up longer, either briefly meet with and apologize to your guest or send someone else to apologize for you. Going out in person is the best choice. This will set a warm and welcoming tone for your upcoming meeting. Let the guest know that it will only be a few more minutes. Offer water, coffee, or a magazine if the wait will be more than a few more minutes.

If your guest is late, accept the apology graciously. If it is so late that you are unable to meet, accept the apology in person, but try to work the visitor in if at all possible. Things do happen that delay well meaning people.

If you will be meeting with a guest or other visitor, let the property switchboard operator and team members know that you are in a meeting and calls will need to be forwarded. Turn off your cell phone.

Hotels and other organizations devote their best spaces to client meeting and reception areas, ballrooms, dining rooms, or guest rooms, and any other areas that will generate income. So your office or cubicle may not be well suited for a visit with a guest or a client. Reserve a meeting or conference room if you work in a cube or in a small office. You may want to meet with your guest in the lobby or coffee shop, as appropriate. The important thing is to be courteous and to make your guest as comfortable as possible.

If the guest is not familiar with the property, then well before the meeting, e-mail or fax clear driving directions and parking instructions. Follow up with a telephone call to make sure that the directions were received and are understood. Remember to include information about parking areas or valet services. If the guest will be using your valet services, let this person know ahead of time if the property or organization is taking care of the parking fees.

Meet your guest in the lobby. If the meeting is not in the lobby, walk your visitor to the meeting location. You will either walk by your guest's side (your guest is on your right) or it may be necessary to lead your guest through any narrow inside passageways and up or down stairs. Let your visitor know when you need to take the lead. If your guest has an umbrella, coat, or raincoat, when you reach your destination take these items and store them appropriately. Your guest will enter the meeting room in front of you. When deciding where and how to properly seat your guest, consider the following:

- Show your visitor where to sit. There may be couches and chairs, or two or more chairs on the same side of a desk.
- Sit in the same area in which you have seated your guest. Sitting behind your desk could make you appear separated from or cold toward your guest.
- If you are both at a conference table, seat your guest to your right or directly across from you.
- You may take the seat at the head of the table.
- If you are receiving more than one guest from another organization, the highest ranking member of that team sits at the center of the conference table, facing the door, with other team members seated alongside of him or her.
- When you receive as a team, then your team sits directly opposite your guest's team, with your most senior official seated across from the other senior official.

If you know that the meeting will take longer than fifteen minutes, be prepared to offer your guest(s) water, coffee, or tea. If you are able to use real china cups instead of paper cups, you will make a much stronger impression. Your team's handbags, tote bags, and briefcases are never placed on a conference table or on a desk. Electronics may be placed on a conference table or desk if being used as part of a presentation or if your team members are using their tablets, laptops, electronic notepads, and/or other devices to take notes.

See your visitor(s) back to the lobby or parking area. Remember to follow up as appropriate after the appointment. This may be in the form of a written note or report, e-mail, or other action you agreed to take during the meeting.

CHILDREN ON PROPERTY

The etiquette of assisting a parent or caregiver on property or other company location begins with knowing to never touch a child. Do not give a child candy or any food or beverage without first asking the parent or caregiver if you may do so.

Small children generally do not have long attention spans. Many hotel brands offer family oriented entertainment, nannies, and babysitting services. I recommend that both the concierge's desk and the coffee shop or restaurant have the tools necessary to assist frazzled parents in toning down small guests. Coloring books and crayons, or even a brightly colored collection of building blocks set up in a quiet area in anticipation of such a storm, are excellent distractions.

Suggest to your general manager that the property have on hand a boxful of inexpensive stuffed animals to give to crying or screaming children as a distraction. A soft and furry giraffe will almost always stop both the tears and the noise. Always first ask the parent or caregiver if you may distract the child in this way.

Toys cannot have any parts that can be removed or swallowed (eyes, bow ties, button noses). Smile, speak in a soothing voice, give out the toy or coloring book after receiving the parent's permission to do so, offer a predetermined quiet area, or ask how you may assist.

PETIQUETTE

Distracting a yapping pet is very similar to calming down a toddler. Smile and speak in a soothing voice. Have some treats on hand at the concierge's desk. Always ask permission before petting or feeding a guest's animal.

If the animal commits an ungracious mistake in the lobby, quietly and immediately call housekeeping. While the dog's mom or dad is busy apologizing, offer to show the guest where, outside, the offending pup may be walked. If you are exiting to escort the guest (and dog) to a grassy area, leave an associate standing guard by the stain until housekeeping arrives. Call the dog butler if your property has one.

If there are complaints from other guests about a dog barking in a guest room, call the dog's owners and let them know that you have received a call from another guest. Ask what you may do to assist them with their pet. Offer to walk Rasputin or bring up some treats.

Have a medium sized soft rubber dog toy available for these dire situations. Small toys can be swallowed. This toy cannot have any parts that can be removed or swallowed (eyes, bow ties, button noses). Sometimes the animal is just bored.

CELEBRITIES

Your property or organization attracts celebrities because you have earned a reputation for quality and respect for the privacy of your guests. The number one rule when receiving celebrities is to respect their privacy. I know that you would never consider asking for an autograph, nor would you ask if he or she would let you take a photograph. You will always keep your distance, especially if the celebrity has brought his or her family during this stay.

Remember that celebrities are protective of their children, so be very mindful that there may be bodyguards, nannies, and/or private tutors in the entourage. You need to speak directly with these people or with the parents; never approach a celebrity's child directly.

Always address these guests in the same way that you would address all guests, by using the correct title: Mr., Mrs., Ms., Dr., Father, etc. By all means, if you are working with this person, introduce yourself and briefly shake hands, using appropriate eye contact and being aware not to stand inappropriately close to the celebrity.

Should you ever be introduced to the Queen of England, know that she is initially addressed as "Your Majesty." Thereafter, you will address her as "Ma'am." Never offer her your hand. If she wants to shake your hand, she will do so. Never curtsey or bow unless you are a subject of the United Kingdom.

The president of the United States is addressed as "Mr. President." Thereafter, you will address him as "Sir." A female United States president would be addressed as "Madame President." Thereafter you would address her as "Ma'am." Either you will be introduced to the president by an aide or the president will introduce himself. Allow the president to extend his hand first.

In conversation, address the president of a foreign republic as either "Your Excellency" or "Mr. President."

MEDICAL TOURISM

Most of your guests choose to visit your property, fly your airline, or cruise on your ships for reasons of either business or pleasure. Some tourists may travel with you and then stay at a hotel while recovering from an elective or a complex and specialized medical procedure. This stay is part of a growing trend worldwide called *medical tourism.*

While a typical medical tourist may be visiting while recovering from cosmetic surgery, virtually any type of health care may be involved. North American medical tourists travel abroad to receive care. Because of the availability of advanced technology and specialized physician training, the fastest growing group of global medical travelers is finding its way to the United States (Wikipedia 2013). Airlines are becoming very familiar with this trend.

These guests are staying with you because they need the privacy, quiet, and excellent service that you will provide. Many medical tourists have a nursing assistant staying with them. The assistant will answer the guest room door to receive flowers, food, and other deliveries.

You may see these guests in the halls or elevators as they are escorted, either on foot or in a wheelchair, to their transportation, or to their rooms following a medical procedure. They may appear bruised, bandaged, and battered. They will not feel well. They will not feel sociable. They may be embarrassed by their appearance. This is the only situation in which I will advise that you try to stay away from a guest if at all possible. Avoid direct eye contact.

Continue on your way. Never ask this guest any questions. Simply say "Good morning" and keep walking.

DISRUPTIVE GUESTS

It is unfortunate, but it may happen that the commitment and respect that you hold for your guests will be tried dearly. From time to time, a guest may behave badly. A couple may raise their voices to each other in a public area. I am now speaking about a disagreement and raised voices, not a violent confrontation. This situation, while partially about etiquette, has two other parts. One part is sensitivity toward these guests, and the other is the safety and comfort of yourself, your associates, and your other guests.

If you are unable or unauthorized to handle this situation, quickly find your team leader or other member of management. If the situation must be addressed immediately, and you are authorized to do so, go to the guests and say (while smiling), "Excuse me, I'm so sorry to interrupt, but since there are so many other guests in the lobby, I have to ask that you please lower your voices. Again, I'm so sorry I've interrupted you."

A similar situation may occur where one or both parties have been drinking. Immediately call security if alcohol or any other questionable substance is involved or if you believe there is the potential for physical violence. A member of the security team will take over in these situations. Check your operations manual for guidance in these and any potentially harmful guest related situations.

CHAPTER 11

The Power of Your Wardrobe
Clothes and Grooming Talk

Your guests are listening with their eyes. The right choices in clothing, accessories, and grooming will communicate trust and credibility whether you are working (or playing) locally or abroad. All you really need to know is how to dress to communicate excellence. Style is nice but substance is better. The term *universal standards* is used when discussing first class grooming in the hospitality management arena.

CLOTHING

Wear only clothes made of good quality fabrics. If an article of clothing is very inexpensive, it may look cheap when you wear it, and it will lose its shape quickly. It is better to invest in just a few very good pieces of clothing at a time. Less is more. You can always add pieces as your budget permits.

Make friends with the personal shopper at your local department store. Let him or her know that you are building a professional wardrobe. This person will call you when appropriate wardrobe pieces and accessories are going on sale.

Suits, jackets, and sport coats add not only distinction but also the look of competence. Allow one-half inch of your shirt cuff to be visible below the sleeve of your suit. Make sure that your clothes have straight lines—no ruffles or flounces. Ruffles take away from your credibility.

Colors

Psychology experts tell us that blue tones—such as navy, dark blue, and royal blue—project trust. For men, wearing brown can cause mistrust. This is not true for women. Navy and black are absolutely the best professional colors. These are followed by rich shades of green, red, brown, and taupe (Maysonave 1999). Dark charcoal grey is another excellent choice. Your clothes should not be trendy; avoid loud colors.

Generally, hospitality professionals do not wear clothes that are provocative. Skirts must not be too short and tops must never show what shouldn't be shown. Your guests must be taken with your kindness and competence, not a show of skin or cleavage. The rule is that the more skin you show, the less seriously you will be taken as a professional. Provocative uniforms may be the standard for some ultra casual bar, tropical, or bistro type establishments.

Short-sleeved shirts are generally not worn in the hospitality field unless they are a part of a uniform or the property is situated in a tropical location. For both men and women, short-sleeved shirts take away from your position of authority. In extremely warm climates, some brands allow men and women in management to wear short-sleeved shirts. Even so, jackets may be put on for business meetings and during client interactions.

We all gain and lose weight. As a hospitality professional, this is never an excuse for wearing clothes that are very loose or too tight. You are a polished professional. Invest in yourself; invest in a tailor when you need one. Your clothes must be well tailored, pressed, and spotless.

Undergarments

Women, visit the lingerie section of your local department store. Have your foundation garments fitted to your body by a professional. How well your undergarments fit will determine how well your clothes look on you. Men, consider how you look in your suit or uniform. You may want to wear an undershirt if perspiration is an issue for you.

ACCESSORIES

Your watch is your most noticed accessory and is a symbol of status and efficiency. This is your one most important purchase. Invest in a classic and sophisticated timepiece; avoid digital watches unless you are on your way to a workout at the gym.

Your next most visible accessory is your pen. Your guests will notice your writing implement. It cannot be a felt-tipped pen. For the present, use your brand's pen with the logo. When you are able, invest in an excellent pen that is in keeping with your quality wardrobe. Keep your pen in your portfolio, with your clipboard, or in an inside jacket pocket, never in your shirt pocket. Pens kept in shirt pockets are for order takers. Your guest expects a hospitality professional, not a clerk.

You will carry either a portfolio or an attaché case (also called a briefcase) to meetings. The more supple the leather and the less your attaché case or portfolio bulges, the more competent and in charge you will look. Attaché and portfolio power colors are black or brown. Unless issued to you by your property or considered a part of your uniform, personal cell phones, Bluetooth headsets, and other electronic items must not be visible while you are working.

Your shoes say a lot about you. Your guests and others will look at your shoes the moment that they finish assessing your hair and face. Shoes help you to feel confident and look pulled together. Invest in two pairs of very good black (or another neutral color that goes with your wardrobe) shoes that you can rotate.

For men, the basic black leather oxford is an excellent choice. This shoe has between three and six eyelets and will take you right from work to a cocktail reception. You can add to your professional shoe wardrobe as your budget permits. Keep your shoes polished, heeled, and soled. Shabby looking shoes scream bad performer!

Your brand's dress code will specify whether or not hosiery is required when wearing a dress or a skirt at your property. In addition to tropical and more casual properties, many brands no longer require women to wear hosiery in the workplace. Should you be required to wear hosiery, keep the colors sheer nude, sheer black, or opaque black. Your hose may be lighter, but never darker than, your shoe.

For women, sling-back and open-toed shoes are not professional footwear and may pose a safety risk on property. Check your dress code before spending money on shoes that may not be appropriate.

Wear very simple, high quality jewelry. One piece of jewelry makes a well-dressed statement. Professional women will never wear more than one ring on each hand. A combined wedding band and engagement ring worn on one finger are considered as one ring. Men in hospitality must never wear neck chains.

Men, your belts must be of fine quality leather. They must be well-maintained. Women, invest in one high quality black handbag. I suggest a shoulder bag. This is a versatile piece that carries a message of competence. You can wear this every day with all of your work outfits. It is easy to travel with and to have on your shoulder when you are at a business reception and need to shake hands with your right hand and hold a cocktail glass in your left.

GROOMING

You are squeaky clean. You shower or bathe each day. You use a deodorant or antiperspirant. You are impeccably groomed. You brush your teeth at least twice a day, and you floss your teeth daily. You rinse with mouthwash. Keep an extra toothbrush and a tube of toothpaste at work. Your guests (and fellow associates) should never notice your breath.

Your smile is a huge asset in this industry. See a dentist regularly, and if you feel that your teeth could be brighter or straighter, discuss this with your dentist. Even if you are on a budget, your dentist will have options for accomplishing your goals.

Regarding your physical characteristics, your guests will first look at your hair to learn about your cleanliness and general public presentation. Have your hair professionally styled. Unless your brand is exceptionally trendy or hip, long hair must be pulled back neatly, away from your face. Most brands want hair to fall no lower than the collarbone. Remember to regularly touch up dyed roots that may be showing. Dark roots against light hair can sabotage your look of being put together elegantly and professionally.

You know not to play with or touch your hair in public. This will undermine your look of confidence. It may look like you are flirting with your guest. For male employees, facial hair is cause for mistrust in many cultures. If your brand allows mustaches and beards, these must be kept immaculately trimmed (Maysonave 1999).

Men, make sure that nose and ear hair are trimmed. Purchase a trimmer for this grooming activity or have your barber take care of it.

To be taken seriously, both men and women must have well cared for nails and cuticles. If regular manicures are not currently in your budget, learn how to give yourself a weekly manicure. Women in hospitality wear neutral or light shades of nail polish. Some properties located in more trendy cities allow darker shades of nail polish. Check your brand's policy. Nails are to be kept short or of medium length. Never appear in public if your nail polish is chipped or does not look freshly applied.

Studies show that women who wear makeup earn incomes up to 20 to 30 percent higher than women who do not (Maysonave 1999). Avoid frosty eye shadows. They are more club than office. Have a professional at your local cosmetics counter show you how to apply makeup with a light touch. He or she will help you select makeup that compliments your skin tone and features.

Never wear more than a touch of cologne or perfume. Some guests and even your associates may be sensitive to fragrance. When in doubt, do not wear fragrance.

The professional who has tattoos and/or body piercings (other than ear piercings for one set of small earrings) must keep these covered unless he or she is working in an extremely casual or trendy restaurant or at a very hip and fashion forward property. Check your brand's dress code.

Both men and women need to look at themselves in a full length mirror prior to leaving home. Check your shoulders for dandruff and your suit or other attire for lint. Keep one lint brush in your car and another at work, in your locker or desk.

UNIFORMS

Uniforms are worn to send a message to your guests. You are saying, "I am recognizable and competent, and I am here to serve you. Please approach me." When you wear your uniform with pride, a guest will see you as essential (Michael 2000).

As with any other wardrobe accessories, keep jewelry to an understated minimum. Rings and bracelets may interfere with your work or pose a safety risk. At orientation, your brand will tell you what specific accessories are appropriate for your uniform. Check your employee handbook to be sure that you are wearing required brand pins.

Review your dress code and purchase shoes that are appropriate for your work. You must be comfortable and you must be safe. Wear socks or hose that blend with your shoes and slacks or skirt. Dark socks go with dark shoes. Gentlemen, always check your socks for holes. Make sure that they are not worn thin. Ladies, look in the mirror before leaving home. Are there any runs in your hose?

Uniforms must fit comfortably. Guests will notice if the uniform seems either too tight or too loose. The skirt hemline of your professional uniform should be no higher than the top of your knee unless a shorter uniform is appropriate to your brand or to the job you perform. Carefully look at yourself from all angles (front and back) in a full length mirror to make sure that your undergarments are not visible through your uniform.

Your uniform will look outstanding if it is always cleaned and pressed. It must be free of stains, spots, and odors. Replace missing buttons right away. Fix falling hems on skirts and trousers.

Everything in our prior discussion about good grooming applies to the associate proudly wearing a hospitality uniform. Don't forget to wear your name tag on the side of your clothing and in the location designated by your brand. Unless issued to you by your property, personal cell phones, Bluetooth headsets, and other electronic items are not a part of your official uniform. Do not carry these items while working. Large personal items, such as combs, need to be kept in your locker.

Before interacting with guests and fellow associates, look carefully at your overall professional image in a mirror.

DRESSING WHEN OUT AND ABOUT

Your business and social life will continue to offer a variety of exciting occasions. On one hand, you may receive an invitation to the wedding of your general manager's daughter. There you are, wondering what *black tie optional* means, or puzzling over the difference between *business casual* and *business appropriate*. Cracking the business and social dress code isn't all that difficult. Just review the few basic terms, definitions, and suggestions found below.

White Tie

If your invitation has the words *white tie* printed on the lower righthand corner, you have been invited to an ultra formal ball, opera, or even a diplomatic affair. Men generally rent the required black tailcoat, white vest, and white tie. Women wear floor length gowns, gloves, and their best jewelry.

Black Tie

You may receive an invitation that has the words *black tie* printed on the lower right hand corner. This means that men wear a tuxedo and women wear either a floor length dress, cocktail dress, fine looking evening suit, or fancy trouser outfit.

A corsage is a small arrangement of flowers given to a lady as a gift to mark an important occasion. While not as popular as in the past, at a black tie wedding, the mothers of the bride and groom along with a few special relatives and friends may receive corsages. The corsage is worn at formal affairs on a woman's left wrist or pinned to her dress either on her left upper chest or at the waist. A woman may pin a corsage onto her evening bag to avoid a pin mark on her cocktail dress or formal gown.

Corsages are a traditional gift to high school prom dates. The corsage dates back to medieval times when most people did not bathe regularly. Flowers were worn to mask unpleasant odors. Today the corsage is a lovely decoration.

Black Tie Optional

The female guest will dress in the same manner as she would for a black tie affair. It's up to the male guest to decide if he will wear a tuxedo or not. A man may choose not to wear a tuxedo. If that's the case, he'll want to invest in one very good, well-tailored dark suit. He will wear this suit to the affair with a white shirt and conservative tie. Traditionally, this one investment suit is black, but etiquette does evolve. Other options are impeccably tailored suits in dark navy or charcoal.

Tuxedo Tutorial

Never wear a tuxedo to a function that is scheduled before six in the evening. Tuxedos are worn with a white formal shirt, a black bow tie, and a cummerbund that fits around the waist. The classic shirt may be either plain or pleated. Do not wear a shirt that has ruffles on it. This would not only seem in bad taste but will also place your fashion sense firmly in the 1970s.

The gentleman wears matching studs and cuff links with his tuxedo shirt. Studs are made like tiny cuff links. They have a small bar in back that goes through an open buttonhole and holds the stud in place; the stud holds the shirt closed. A tuxedo shirt has a regular button at the top and another regular button at the bottom. There are four buttonless buttonholes in between. This is where the decorative studs go.

The man wears black patent pumps or black patent laced oxfords with lightweight black tuxedo socks. Make sure the socks fit over the calf. Some men like to wear a cummerbund and a tie in a bright color or a more modern fabric, such as silk or velvet. A cummerbund is a broad waist sash. It is usually horizontally pleated. Tuxedo vests are another fashionable option.

If you are a groomsman in a formal wedding party, you will be given a boutonniere to wear. You pronounce this *"bootneer."* This is a single flower or bud that is pinned onto the left lapel of your tuxedo. Boutonniere is from the French meaning buttonhole. The British still call this floral decoration a *buttonhole* because the flower was pushed through a lapel buttonhole that had a special stem loop sewn onto the back. Today, most tuxedos are not designed with the original lapel stem loop.

Tuxedos can be rented or purchased, as can the shoes. If your brand and/or lifestyle does not demand that you attend a large number of formal affairs, then confidently rent up-to-date tuxedos as you need them. Many men who do attend a fair number of these events prefer to purchase their own comfortable shoes and socks while continuing to rent their tuxedos.

Cocktail Attire

Also known as *after five*, this dress code means that gentlemen wear a dark suit and a smart tie, generally with a white shirt for a classic look. Ladies wear short, elegant dresses. Very stylish evening pants or skirts and chic, dressy tops are also appropriate for women. In the past, this dress option was known as *semiformal*. Please think about what sort of guests you will be meeting at this party when you are considering exactly how short your cocktail dress or skirt will be. If the cocktail party is strictly a business affair that you are attending right after work, then both men and women will attend in corporate dress, which is discussed below.

Corporate Dress

Corporate dress means that men wear a suit and tie, generally with a white shirt. Depending on the formality of your property, optional shirt colors may include light blue and pale pink. Women wear suits as well. Corporate dress is the most formal business dress code and is the standard for trust companies, investment banks, and most law firms (Gross and Stone 2002).

For men, if your suit has three buttons, always make sure that the top two are buttoned when you are standing, and if the suit has two buttons, make sure the top button is buttoned when standing. Your tie should be long enough to reach your belt. A professional tie will be solid in color or have a stripe or small pattern on it.

Business Casual

This code is more relaxed, and jackets are not necessary for men or women. However, a shirt (not a T-shirt) or sweater is compulsory. Mix a traditional business item with something more casual. Consider wearing a jacket and no tie. You need to be dressed in such a way that you never feel uncomfortable if you should run into the CEO or a client. In hospitality, this code is not the norm, but it can be found at a very casual property or dining establishment or at a property located in the tropics.

Casual

The days of dot-com, tie-dyed casual are over. Casual at work means no T-shirts without a jacket and no T-shirts bearing logos or sayings. No item of clothing can be cut, faded, ripped, or hanging (Gross and Stone 2002). Jeans and a jacket are acceptable, but this type of casual is better left for going out to dinner with friends. In all but the most low-key hospitality settings, this code is close to nonexistent.

Smart Casual

Also called *elegant casual* and *casual chic*, this code is best for informal cocktail parties in hotels and private homes and dining in very good restaurants. Men wear a jacket and shirt, no tie. Women wear casual but elegant dresses or smart pants and tops or other chic outfits. There are some resorts in tropical locations where managers have adopted this dress code.

Business Appropriate

This is the dress code you will be shooting for if your position does not require a uniform. This code is about dressing appropriately for your position, what you do every day, those you meet, and more importantly, those you may meet. For men and women, this code begins with the knowledge that a jacket is mandatory. Depending on your brand and position, a suit may be necessary as well (Gross and Stone 2002).

If a suit is not necessary, men wear a sports jacket with a tie and women wear their jackets over a dress or tailored trousers. Some brands may require heels, and some still require hose for women's business appropriate attire. Open-toed shoes may not be a part of your business dress code. Check your brand's dress code policy for appropriateness.

CHAPTER 12

Your Public Behavior
Your Life Outside of Work

You have a life outside of work. Play hard and have a great time. This section of the book reinforces the rules of kindness and exemplary behavior that extend to the mall, the gym, and anywhere else where people will judge you, on or off the clock.

GOLF ETIQUETTE

The game of golf began in Scotland over five hundred years ago. The King of Scotland, James VI, brought the game to England when he succeeded to the English throne in 1603 (Tour Canada 1996). It has, throughout its history, been a game of both skill and honor. Never try to fake your golfing abilities. If you are truly interested in this celebrated game, take lessons. You will find your improved golfing skills to be invaluable in both your business and social lives.

Dress appropriately for the game. No jeans, T-shirts, or gym shoes. Golf shirts and either long shorts or long pants are appropriate. I suggest a hat or visor to protect you from the heat and from sunburn.

The host chooses the golf course. The course may be at a country club where the host is a member. The guest needs to let the host know his or her golfing ability so the host can put together a suitable foursome based on ability. Be mindful of other people when swinging your club. Warn other players by yelling "Fore" if you think your ball may hit them.

If there is a group ahead of you, try to keep pace. Allow a faster player to play through. Par is the ideal number of strokes needed to complete a hole. One stroke less than par is called a birdie and two less is called an eagle. Never give advice on how to play a hole unless someone asks for it.

Do not use electronics on the golf course. Do not talk business on the links. This can wait until your guest brings up the subject, either on the links or after the game. Leave enough time for a drink or snack on the "19th hole"—slang for the bar at the club house.

If you are the guest, a thank-you note or short thank-you letter is appropriate. Minimally, a thank-you telephone call is mandatory. Depending on the relationship, a gift may be correct, or you may reciprocate by hosting a round of golf on another day. Generally, you will not be able to offer your host lunch, dinner, or a drink if you are not a member of the country club.

GYM ETIQUETTE

Sign in at the front desk and please dress appropriately. In the gym, you need to have on clothes that are comfortable and cool yet don't show us any part of you that generally shouldn't be seen.

Bring a hand towel along and wipe your perspiration off the machines and mats that you have used. Obey the gym's rules regarding the amount of time you can spend on various machines. Offer to rotate your workout with members who are waiting to use the machines. After using the equipment, please put back the weights, balls, and other items you've removed from their shelves and brackets. It is considerate to reset the weight machines you have been using.

Don't be late if you have scheduled either a personal or a group fitness session. Limit your use of perfumes, colognes, and hair spray in the locker room, as other members may be affected because of allergies or other medical conditions. There will be a hamper for used towels and receptacles for paper items. Remember to clean up after yourself in the showers and dressing areas.

Absolutely no cell phone use or texting in the gym or locker room. We are concentrating on our workouts, and your constant chatter, ring tone, or key tapping is distracting and impolite.

Cell phones are equipped with cameras, so by policy, most brands and most fitness corporations do not allow cell phones in gyms or locker rooms. Gym guests are often celebrities and other public figures seeking privacy. They will not want to see their picture in gym shorts appearing in a tabloid.

MOVIE THEATER ETIQUETTE

In movies theaters, please remove your sports cap so that I can see the show. All electronic devices must be turned off—even for texting, which the people to your right, your left, and behind you can see. This is annoying. Please don't whisper or talk throughout the show, and try not to crinkle your candy wrappers too much. If you have a problem with others, ask an usher to take care of it.

OPERA, BALLET, AND SYMPHONY ETIQUETTE

Please arrive on time and don't dash out before the end of the performance. This can throw off the performers and distract the audience. An usher may escort you to your seats. He or she will lead. It is traditional for the woman to enter the row first.

If you arrive late, never attempt to find your seat after the opera, ballet, or symphony has begun. Wait for an usher to escort you to your seat. In North America, we turn our backs to those already seated as we enter our rows. In Europe, face those already seated when entering your row.

Applaud when the conductor enters at symphonies, operas, and ballets. You will also applaud after the last note is played at a symphony, not before. The curtain will rise and fall during the performance, but do not applaud. At an Italian opera, it is acceptable to applaud after arias. The word *aria* is Italian for "air." It is a word that describes a piece of music for one voice, usually accompanied by an orchestra (Wikipedia 2012).

You would not applaud at a German opera until the last note is played. Take your cues from the experts in your party.

As in movie theaters, please no whispering, talking, or electronics. Please don't wear bangle bracelets or other jewelry that makes noise. Your cell phone is turned off; it must not ring during the performance. Try to be as still as possible during a performance.

SHOPPING ETIQUETTE

The old "you'll catch more flies with honey than vinegar" saying is again useful and will be your guide to a great shopping experience. Show extra courtesy to employees. It can't be easy working at a mall, retail store, or grocery.

Do not use a cell phone when speaking with an employee or making your purchase. Do not speak on your cell phone while giving your order to that nice lady in the deli section. Other customers are behind you, and there you are, holding us all hostage to your cell phone conversation. If you must use your cell phone while shopping, please keep your voice low and try to keep a ten-foot distance between you and the nearest shopper.

Take your credit card, cash, or check out as you approach the cash register. Please don't keep the rest of us waiting while you examine the entire contents of your pocketbook, wallet, or fanny pack. You may need to relax and be patient if there is a line of people ahead of you at the register. You will need to be patient if there is a customer ahead of you who is slow because of a handicap.

Be mindful of your shopping bags, and be aware that there are many people around you who might either get hit by your bags or attempt to take one of your bags. Keep your purse closed and be wary of pickpockets.

Children do not have the same patience at shopping malls and grocery stores that you do. Take snacks for the children and, if possible, take a helper so that someone is paying close attention to the children.

If you're in a checkout line, it's still polite to let the shopper who is behind you with only one or two items go first.

Never leave your cart in the center of the shopping aisle; there are other people in the store. In North America, walk on the right side of the shopping aisle only. Push your grocery cart on the right side only. Always park your shopping cart on the right of the aisle. The opposite is true in Europe.

SPA ETIQUETTE

A spa is a place of quiet relaxation. This means no cell phones or beepers—in fact, no electronics of any kind. This also means that you will not take your children with you to the spa out of respect for other guests who are looking forward to a quiet retreat.

Make your treatment appointments early so that you get the time slot you prefer and your choice of therapists. If you must cancel, please do so as much in advance as possible. Some spas have cancellation fees, so check on this when booking your appointment.

Let the spa receptionist know ahead of time if you are pregnant so that you can be kept safe and made more comfortable. There are various spa treatments that are not advisable for mothers-to-be, so speak up.

Arriving at a spa on time means that you are late. Arrive between fifteen and thirty minutes prior to your first scheduled treatment. You will be given a tour of the spa and shown to your locker. You will be given a locker key. The locker room is where you change into a spa robe for a treatment. This is a great time to ask questions about the steam room, sauna, and/or hot tub.

When booking appointments, ask the receptionist what amenities are available for your use. Most spas have hair dryers, flat irons, and curling irons, shampoos, conditioners, hair spray, deodorant, razors, and a variety of other items available at no additional cost for your use. It is suggested that women do not shave for twenty-four hours prior to certain treatments. Men are asked to shave before facial treatments. Speak with the receptionist about this when booking your treatments.

Never bring food into the day spa. Your attendants will be happy to bring you refreshing beverages; often, you will find fruit and other healthful snacks available to you without charge. Spas generally offer a menu from which you may order your lunch or other meal. The cost of this meal will be added to your spa bill.

It's all right to request a male or a female massage therapist. Everyone has a different comfort level, so be sure to find out what, if anything, you're expected to wear for different treatments. Wear whatever makes you comfortable. There may be both nudity and people wearing bathing suits in the sauna, steam room, and hot tubs.

Some spas have small safes located inside of the individual lockers. If your locker has a small safe, then you will be given a key for the safe. Locker and safe keys are worn on a plastic wrist bracelet. I advise that you not bring jewelry or large amounts of cash to a spa. You will not need cash, as you earlier confirmed your reservation with either a credit card or your room number.

Do not be shy about telling a therapist if your treatment is not to your liking. Be kind. Explain exactly what the problem is so that it can be immediately corrected. Do not wait until the treatment is finished to speak up.

Many spas have a quiet room. Guests may wait in this room to be called for their treatment. Or it may be a place to have tea and quietly read a book. This area is for whispering only, no loud conversations. Absolutely no cell phones or cameras anywhere in the spa.

In chapter 7, I discussed tipping guidelines. Generally 20 percent is the customary gratuity, depending on level of service. You may, of course, leave more or less. Review your spa bill carefully; often a gratuity of up to 22 percent is already added into your total. Separate tips are left for each person who gave you a treatment.

The tip, if you are not adding it to your bill, will be left at the reception desk in an envelope with your therapist's name written on it.

TENNIS COURT ETIQUETTE

Tennis originated as a 12th-century French game called *paume,* which means "palm." The ball was hit back and forth with the palm of a gloved hand. The nobility learned the game from monks. In 16th-century England, the glove became a racquet, the game was moved to an enclosed indoor area, and rules of play were formalized. Soon, the wooden tennis racquet made its debut and was widely used. Charles Goodyear invented vulcanized rubber in 1850, so now tennis balls actually bounced (Cooper 2013)! By the 1800s, tennis had become well-known and popular worldwide.

Whether you are playing at a country club, public courts, or a private home, respect and courtesy are the basics of the game of tennis. Dress appropriately as a show of respect for the game, your partner, and your opponents. It goes without saying that you will wear proper tennis shoes on the court.

When you arrive at the court, check the rules that the tennis site has posted. Never interrupt games on neighboring courts. If you must retrieve a lost ball, wait until the point is over. You know to wait until your opponent is ready before you serve. If a ball from another court interrupts your game, call a "let" ball.

Remember to keep your voice down. If there is a disagreement, you must take this discussion off the court and away from other players and spectators. Clean up after yourself so that the next players are not welcomed by your empty soda cans and candy wrappers.

Children will love to watch you play. Make sure that another adult is watching your children closely while you are playing. This is both for their own safety and for the enjoyment of adult players and spectators (Eggers 2012). Enjoy the game.

UNATTRACTIVE HABITS

At work or play, on the street or in any public place, you are being watched by friends, colleagues, management, potential employers, and the public at large. Some personal behaviors will make you appear unprofessional, disrespectful, or uneducated.

Chewing Gum

Chewing gum in public is disrespectful. This is especially true if you are speaking one-on-one with a coworker or guest. Worse still is chomping away while conducting either a business or personal telephone conversation. No one can understand you. If you must chew, do so on the way to work or on the way home. Try this: put a stick (or two) of gum in your mouth and watch in the mirror as you chew. Not very attractive, is it? Always dispose of your gum in a tissue.

Smoking

Most companies and most countries, states, and cities have laws that govern when, where, and what you may smoke. A good rule in both your business and social life is that if you don't see an ashtray, don't ask for one. Even if it is allowed, never smoke at a table while others are eating. When conducting business, even if it is allowed, just don't smoke. If you must, then excuse yourself and go outside.

Smoking separates you from your team, family, and friends. Many brands offer smoke cessation programs or will reimburse you for successfully completing a program. Investigate this healthful alternative.

Candy

Crunching, chewing, and sucking on candy or mints is not the mark of a true professional. It is very distracting to the person who is standing right in front of you. I carry an energy bar or raisins in my briefcase so that I can avoid candy if it is offered. When I miss lunch because I must meet a client for business or a friend for shopping, I have a healthful snack before our meeting.

Never eat in the public view unless you are in a restaurant, at a friendly gathering, or at a picnic. Chewing on ice while dining is similarly distracting behavior.

Toothpicks

Toothpicks have no place at a dining table. Toothpicks date back to prehistoric times and have an interesting place in history.

Archeologists have unearthed toothpicks made of bone, ivory, quills, and wood. Early man used his teeth to tear his raw dinner to bits. As he had neither dentists nor dental floss, toothpicks were central to oral hygiene. In China, many adults still use toothpicks at the dining table. The younger, more global Chinese generation is moving away from this practice.

You will notice that some casual restaurants do offer toothpicks. They are placed by the cash register so that you may take one on your way out of the restaurant. Never pick up a toothpick on your way out of a restaurant after a business meal. Fair or not, business associates (and the rest of us) watch you and judge you by your actions. Absolutely never use a toothpick in public.

CHAPTER 13

Dining Etiquette
Business and Social Dining

Business and social relationships are developed and strengthened at the table. In addition to dining at your property with guests, this expectation extends to dining out socially with family and friends. The real point is that you should be so comfortable at the table that no one actually notices your dining talents. Besides actual knowledge and common sense, great observation skills and a sense of humor are required when dining or serving.

In this chapter, you will find business and social dining skills information that is both modern and timeless. Enjoy.

AT THE TABLE

I'm guessing that your mother told you to "start with the utensils toward the outside of the plate and work your way in." Mom was right. Become familiar with various utensils. When looking down at your place setting, think of a BMW. No, not the car—the words **B**read, **M**eal, **W**ater. Your bread plate is on the left, your meal is in the middle, and your liquids are always on your right. Now you never need to worry again about using someone else's water glass.

Your place setting area is called the *cover*, as in, "Charles, we'll be serving 325 covers for the Adams wedding."

How to Secure the Knife and Fork

Adults often grab their forks, knives, and spoons somewhere in the middle of the utensil, as if they were about to throw a spear. This is how a small child would hold a spoon or a fork. The other option is imitating the famous "knifing in the shower" scene of Alfred Hitchcock's classic horror film *Psycho*.

For better form, hold the knife in your right hand and the fork in your left. Reverse the order if you are left-handed. The fork's tines and the knife's blade are pointed down. Your index fingers rest at the necks of the handles. The rest of your fingers are curled around the handles.

How to Cut Food

When cutting your food, hold the knife in your right hand and the fork in your left, tines down. Your index fingers will be at the neck of your fork and knife. Do not overlap the neck by more than one-half inch. The rest of your fingers will be curled around the handles. *No sawing.* Cutting is a firm but effortless motion.

You are an adult. Only tykes and teens who don't know better cut up all of the food on their plates. Cut only one piece of food at a time, because you will be eating only one piece of food at a time.

American Style of Dining

In American dining, cut the food one bite at a time with your fork in the left hand and the knife in the right hand. After cutting one bite, lay the knife across the top of your plate in the 10:20 position. Just visualize a clock. The tip of the blade is pointed directly at the ten on this imaginary clock and the end of the knife's handle is pointed at the four on this imaginary clock.

Next, switch your fork from your left hand to your right hand. With the tines in an upward position, retrieve the one piece of food you have cut, and bring the food to your mouth. Switch the fork back to your left hand, and pick up the knife in your right hand again. Cut another piece of your meat. You may reverse this process if you are left-handed.

When your knife is resting on your plate, make sure that the blade faces inward, toward you, never outward, toward anyone else. Pointing the blade of your knife toward another diner has historically been considered a sign of aggression.

For the rest position in American dining, place both the knife and fork in the imaginary clock's 10:20 position on your plate. The knife is close to the top of the plate, the tip facing toward the clock's ten. The blade of the knife faces you. There is wide spacing between the knife and the fork in the American resting position. The fork is placed tines up. The rest position is used when talking, taking a drink, or lightly blotting your lips with your napkin. The rest position alerts your server that you are not yet finished with your plate.

The finished position is similar, except that the knife and fork are placed very close to one another in the 10:20 position. The knife's blade again faces you. The fork is again placed tines up.

Continental Style of Dining

In Continental dining, cut the food one bite at a time with the fork in your left hand and the knife in your right hand. After cutting one bite, keep the fork in your left hand, tines facing downward. Slowly turn the fork toward you and bring the food to your mouth. After the food has reached your mouth, bring your left hand back to the table. Place the pad of your left hand on the table's edge. Your fork is pointed straight up. You may reverse this process if you are left-handed.

Leave the pad of your right hand on the table when you are bringing food to your mouth with your left hand. The blade of your knife is pointed toward the ceiling. Be very careful not to point the blade of the knife toward your dining companions. This is considered not only rude but a possibly threatening gesture.

While still holding your knife and fork in the upright position, rest the pads of both hands on the edge of the table when you are chewing or making conversation.

When you are dining in the Continental style, the knife may conveniently be used as a pusher on your plate, to assist you in getting food to adhere to the fork.

In Continental dining, you hold both utensils throughout the meal. Point them upward, not out toward other guests. If you wish to rest, cross the fork, tines down, over the knife in the center of the plate, near the rim, like a large *V.* The rest position is used when talking, taking a drink, or lightly blotting your lips with your napkin. The rest position alerts your server that you are not yet finished with your plate.

Etiquette historians tell us that this exaggerated *V* actually represents the Christian cross. European peasants crossed their silverware at the end of each course as a thank-you prayer to God for providing the meal.

The finished position is the clock's 10:20 position. Place the knife and fork close together; the knife is positioned toward the top of the plate with the blade facing you. The fork is to the knife's left; the tines of the fork face down. The finished position for the English is six o'clock (straight up and down). Again, the fork is placed tines down to the left of the knife. The knife's blade faces inward toward the fork.

When to Begin Eating

When the host picks up his or her napkin, this is your signal that the meal has begun. You may then place your napkin in your own lap. Wait until your host lifts his or her fork or spoon and begins to eat before you lift your own fork or spoon. Do not begin to eat bread or rolls. Do not touch any food on the table until your host lifts his or her fork or spoon and begins to eat. If you are the host, you may certainly tell those who have been served first to begin eating even if everyone else is not yet served.

At some dinners, there will be no host for the table. This might occur at a professional society dinner or trade show meeting. Here, the rules are different. At a buffet type of dinner, wait until at least three other people are seated before placing your napkin on your lap and beginning to eat.

If the dinner is served by waitstaff and the table is round and small (six to eight people), it is easy to wait for everyone to be served. For a much larger table, make sure that at least three other people have been served before you begin to eat. If the table is very long, then wait until eight people around you are seated before placing your napkin on your lap. This generally means two diners on either side of you and four people across from you.

Silent Signals for Your Server

Flatware placement may seem like a silly idea at first glance. The point of it is to be able to silently signal your server that you are finished. Or, alternatively, to silently signal your server that you are simply resting and that you are not ready to give up your plate. A properly trained server knows, based on your silverware placement, not to remove your plate when you are temporarily away from the table. Regardless of your flatware placement, the server does not remove any one dinner plate from the table until each person at the table is finished eating. Then, all plates are removed, and the next course is served.

YOUR DINING CUTLERY

Your dining tools are called *cutlery, utensils, silverware,* or *flatware*. The rule is that no more than three forks are placed to the left of a place setting and no more than three knives are placed to the right. This is called the Rule of Three and dates back to the 1700s, when hosts served three courses only. These courses consisted of a minimum of twenty and sometimes up to one hundred different dishes. Guests ate only from those dishes which were closest to them. Obviously, with all of that food on the table, someone created the Rule of Three to cut down on table clutter. This particular rule can be bent when you place a seafood fork angled in the bowl of the soup spoon to the right of the place setting (Von Drachenfels 2000).

With the advent of mass production in the 1800s, everyone could afford forks, and their use became international. Until that time, most folks were either mashing their food and eating it pressed to the blade of a knife or using a spoon or their hands.

The Salad Fork

In North America, salad is usually the first course served. The salad fork is the utensil placed farthest to the left of your place setting. The salad is eaten after the main course in Europe and after very formal meals in North America. In a Continental (European) style place setting, the salad fork is placed to the right of the dinner fork, since the salad comes after the main course.

When in doubt, take your time and observe what your host does. The left tine of the salad fork is extra wide so that you have more leverage when cutting veined and thick leafy lettuce or broad vegetables that can be served in a salad. The salad fork is approximately 6 to 6½ inches in length.

The Seafood or Cocktail Fork

This is a very small (4½ to 5½ inches) and narrow fork. It has a long handle and three short tines. Use this fork to eat seafood served in a shell or a stemmed glass for both formal and informal dining. An *oyster fork* also has three short tines and looks very much like the cocktail fork. It is about three inches long and is used only in informal dining.

The Fish Fork

This unique fork has an extra wide left tine to assist the diner in separating the fish's flesh from the skeleton. When dining Continental style, hold the fish fork in the left hand with the tines facing downward. When dining American style, hold the fish fork in the right hand with the tines facing upward. This fork is approximately 7¼ to 7¾ inches in length and is appropriate to accompany both formal and informal meals.

The Dinner Fork

This fork is larger than the salad fork. In North America, the dinner fork is placed closest to the dinner plate because it is the second fork used during dinner. The salad fork is placed on the outside of the setting because it is used first. In a Continental place setting, the dinner fork is found on the outside of the setting because it is used first. In Continental dining, the salad fork is to the right of the dinner fork because the salad is served last. Remember Mom's rule: "Start with the silverware on the outside of the plate and work your way in."

The North American dinner fork is approximately 7 inches in length. European cutlery is about one-half inch longer.

The Dessert Fork

A true dessert fork has four tines, while a pastry fork has three. Either fork may be from 6 to 7 inches in length. The left tine of the dessert fork is extra wide so that the diner has more leverage in cutting a firm dessert (Von Drachenfels 2000).

The dessert fork may be brought to the table with your dessert course, or it may be preset at the top of your dinner plate with the dessert fork preset just below the dessert spoon. The fork is set with the tines facing to the right. The spoon is set with the bowl facing to the left.

When your dessert course is served, bring the dessert fork down and place it on the table to the left of your dessert plate. Bring the dessert spoon down and place it on the table to the right of your dessert plate. The server may do this for you.

At the end of the meal, whether you have used both utensils or not, place both the dessert fork and spoon on the plate in the 10:20 finished position. The tines of the fork face down and the bowl of the spoon faces up.

If your dessert is served with only a fork, then at the end of this course, place the used fork on the dessert plate, tines up, in the 10:20, finished position. Unused utensils are never left on the table.

The Salad Knife

There is no true salad knife. If you are served a small knife with the salad course, it is most likely a *luncheon knife*. It is 8 to 8¾ inches long to balance well with a luncheon plate, which is 8½ inches in diameter. This knife will be used with the first course, American style, or after the main course, Continental style. The blade is turned inward to face the plate. At formal meals, a dinner knife is provided to cut the salad.

The Fish Knife

The fish knife has a wide blade and a dull edge. The pointed tip is very sharp to make it easy to separate the flesh from the skeleton and to lift the skeleton and individual bones away from the fish itself. Hold it exactly as you would hold a pencil. These knives are about 8¾ inches long and are useful tools for both formal and informal dining.

The Dinner Knife

This is the longest knife in your place setting. American dinner knives are about 9¼ inches long, while Continental dinner knives are about ½ inch longer. This knife is used for eating the main course.

The Steak Knife

This specialized knife is not a regular part of any flatware set. It has a sharp tip and a serrated edge. It is used to cut thick meat and is properly found at informal meals only. It is 8¼ to 9 inches long (Von Drachenfels 2000). Sold in sets, these knives make lovely and well-appreciated gifts.

The Dessert Knife

This, too, is a specialized piece of cutlery and is not a regular part of a flatware set. It is about 8 inches long. Its blade is narrow. If the blade has a rounded tip, the knife is used when sectioning soft desserts. If the tip is pointed, this dessert knife will assist you in cutting and eating firm desserts (Von Drachenfels 2000). It is well worth searching out these beautiful knifes at flea markets and estate sales.

The Fruit Knife

This piece of cutlery is about 6½ to 7¼ inches long. The blade's edge may be serrated. The tip is always pointed and may have a slight curve. Use this specialized utensil for cutting and peeling fresh fruit (Von Drachenfels 2000).

The Soup Spoon

There are two types of soup spoons. The *oval soup spoon* (anywhere from 5¾ to 8¼ inches long) is used when eating soup that has solid pieces like meat, potatoes, vegetables, and grains in it. It is also used informally for chili, stew, and desserts. The soup is eaten (or sipped) from the front of this spoon, since the soup or stew is made of chunks of food. Formally, it is the only spoon laid on the table, and the soup which accompanies it is served in a soup plate, not a soup bowl.

The second type of soup spoon is the *cream soup spoon*. This spoon is approximately 6 inches long and has a round bowl. Pureed or creamed soup is sipped from the side of this spoon.

The Dessert Spoon

The dessert spoon is approximately 7 to 7¼ inches in length and is used in both formal and casual dining. It may be brought to you when the dessert course is served, or it may be preset at the top of your dinner plate just above the dessert fork. The spoon is set with the bowl facing to the left. The fork is set with the tines facing to the right.

As reviewed earlier, in this chapter's section titled "The Dessert Fork," when your dessert course is served, bring the dessert fork down and place it on the table to the left of your dessert plate. Bring the dessert spoon down and place it on the table to the right of your dessert plate. The server may do this for you.

At the end of the meal, whether you have used both utensils or not, place them on your dessert plate in the 10:20 position. The bowl of the spoon faces up and the tines of the fork face down. If your dessert is served with only a spoon, then at the end of this course, place the used spoon on the saucer that is beneath your dessert cup or plate, in the 10:20, finished position. The bowl of the spoon faces up. Unused utensils are never left on the table.

The Iced-Tea or Iced-Beverage Spoon

Iced tea was made popular at the 1904 St. Louis World's Fair. Richard Blechynden, a tea merchant, found it impossible to interest fairgoers in a cup of hot tea during the sweltering summer heat. Resourceful Mr. Blechynden tried serving his tea in glasses with lots of ice, and a trend was born!

There is no such thing as ice tea, and there certainly are no ice-tea spoons, only *iced-beverage* spoons, also known as *iced-tea* spoons. These have a small bowl and a long thin handle and are between 7 and 10 inches in length. Use this piece of silverware to stir sugar in cold beverages served in tall glasses. Iced tea is properly served at lunch only and would never appear at a formal dinner. Iced-beverage spoons are used for informal dining only.

When you are through stirring your iced tea, if your host has not provided a saucer beneath the iced-beverage glass, you must leave the spoon in the glass (being careful not to poke yourself in the eye when you take a drink). Never place your iced-tea spoon on your host's tablecloth.

These spoons are easily confused with *parfait spoons*, which are used for eating ice cream sodas. Parfait spoons have a bowl that is a little deeper and a little wider, and the handle may be a little longer than that of an iced-beverage spoon. You may easily use your iced-beverage spoon as a parfait spoon.

Iced-tea spoons are not always a part of today's sterling silverware place settings. Still, in America's South, no respectable bride could ever imagine being without her indispensable iced-beverage spoons. Most silver parfait spoons and many iced-beverage spoons are antique. If you are fortunate enough to have inherited a set of this beautiful flatware, use it often.

The Teaspoon

You will never properly see a teaspoon in a place setting at a fine dining restaurant. Teaspoons are found only on tables where the service is informal. In those settings, teaspoons will be placed (improperly) to the left of the soup spoon. I have also seen the teaspoon placed (improperly) at the top of the place setting, just above the dinner plate, for stirring after dinner coffee. At fine dining restaurants, this spoon is served when your coffee or tea is brought to the table. The server places the teaspoon on the beverage's saucer, at the back of the tea or coffee cup (in the 10:20 position). The teaspoon is about 5½ to 6¼ inches long.

The Serving Fork and Spoon

The serving fork and spoon each are about 9 or 10 inches long. When serving yourself from a platter, hold the serving fork in your left hand, tines down. With your right hand, hold the serving spoon, bowl up. The food is lifted up from the serving platter with the serving spoon. The serving fork is used to steady the food as you place it on your plate. If the food on the platter is served on toast, make sure that you slide the bowl of the serving spoon under the toast so that the entire portion is lifted onto your plate. Leaving the toast on the platter is impolite.

If the platter has soft food on it, such as a gelatin mold, cut the food with the side of the serving spoon and lift the portion onto your plate. The serving fork is used to steady the food as you place it on your plate. Use the same method to remove vegetables from the serving platter onto your plate.

It is most important to place the serving spoon and fork next to each other on the platter after you have served yourself. The spoon is placed on the right with its bowl up. The fork is placed to the left of the spoon with the tines facing down to make it easy for the next diner to pick up the serving pieces.

The Individual Butter Spreader

There is no such thing as a *butter knife*. Please stop calling it that. There is a butter spreader that is placed on individual bread plates at both formal and informal meals. Use this small knife to butter bread and rolls. The butter spreader is about 5 or 6 inches long.

When the table is set, the butter spreader is placed directly on the bread-and-butter plate, either at the top or on the right side of this little plate. Its blade faces inward, toward the left. At highly formal meals, there may be no bread served, and thus no bread plate or butter spreader to occupy your thoughts.

The Master Butter Spreader

The master butter spreader is also about 5 to 6 inches long. It is placed in a small serving dish that contains pats of butter. This dish is passed around the table (right to left). Using the master butter spreader, take one pat of butter from this small serving plate and place the pat on your individual bread plate. The master butter server is returned to its serving plate before the serving plate is again passed to the right. When you return the master butter spreader to its serving plate and place it in the 10:20 position, make sure that its blade faces inward, toward you.

Chopsticks

Chopsticks are used more than any other dining utensils in the world. Be well prepared for your Asian guests. Hold your chopsticks between your index finger and your thumb. Hold the top stick as you would a pencil. The lower of the two sticks sits in the web of your hand. The top stick will see the most action. The two middle fingers are used to move the top stick. Find a comfortable position to hold your chopsticks, not too far down and not too high up.

It is not polite to point with chopsticks. Never place chopsticks straight up in a bowl of rice or in a soup bowl. This signifies a funeral offering. Crossing chopsticks is considered unlucky.

At a traditional Asian meal, plates of food are placed in the center of the table for everyone. Never eat directly out of a serving plate. Use the "wrong ends" of your chopsticks to take food from the shared, community plate and place the food onto your own plate before eating it with the "right ends" of your chopsticks. Do not take food directly from a fellow diner's chopsticks.

When resting or finished, place the chopsticks across the top of your plate. The tips of the sticks will be facing to the left. At an authentic Asian feast, you will be given a chopstick rest (it usually resembles a very small ceramic or wooden log). When you are not using your chopsticks, place the tips of the chopsticks, side by side, on this small log. The handles of the chopsticks will rest on the table.

A participant at an Asian banquet will hold a bowl of rice up to his or her mouth and push the rice in. Food taken from shared platters is placed on top of the rice in the bowl. Authentic Asian feasts can last up to three hours. Try not to fill up on the first several courses. Some hosts serve up to twelve courses, and it is polite to eat some of each course.

PLATES AND BOWLS

The word *plate* is from the French, and it means "flat." Before the Industrial Revolution, plates came in two sizes, large and medium. At the beginning of the 1800s, the size of a plate was determined by what time of day you used it. Dinner was a hearty meal, so dinner plates were very large. Luncheon plates were smaller to accommodate a smaller meal. Smaller still were the tea plates and breakfast plates. This variety of sizes was standardized by the middle of the 1800s. Today's plates are just slightly larger than their 19th century predecessors (Von Drachenfels 2000).

Dinner Plate

Our ancestors ate with their hands, either directly from food placed on the table itself or from a wooden bowl. During the Middle Ages, the trencher was born. This was three or four day old hard bread sliced horizontally; food was served directly on this hard bread. *Trencher* is from the French, and it means "to slice."

American settlers ate from wooden "trenchers." Europeans were dining on ceramic plates in the 1500s. The Italians were the first to introduce plates with a deep well. Today we call these plates "soup plates," and we use them to serve soup. The French gave us today's dinner plate with a shallow well in the center and an outer flat rim. Today's dinner plates measure between 10 to 11 inches across.

Luncheon Plate

Luncheon plates are smaller than dinner plates, about 9 to 9½ inches across. This is because lunch is generally a smaller and lighter meal than dinner. These plates were used for ladies' luncheons during the 1800s. Today, they may be used at any meal when serving smaller quantities of food.

Salad Plate

The round salad plate is 7 to 7½ inches across, with its European counterpart about one inch larger. Use this versatile dish for either salads or desserts. Salad plates may also be crescent shaped, like the moon. These lovely English made dishes are about 4½ to 6 inches across, and are only used for informal meals (Von Drachenfels 2000). Remember to serve the salad on a dinner plate if the salad is your main course.

Fruit Plate

Fruit is appropriately served at any point during a meal. You will recognize a fruit plate, as it is decorated with, of all things, pictures of fruit! This charming piece of dinnerware is very specialized and is not a part of a new bride's dinner set. The fruit plate is 6 to 8 inches across. While sets of fruit plates can be found in modern department stores, I encourage you to look for these festive beauties in antique shops.

Cheese Plate

Individual cheese plates are used for both casual and formal dining. They are generally decorated with pictures of cheese and may come in a variety of shapes. They are about 7¼ inches across.

Dessert Plate

In the 1700s, the dessert course involved many different types of desserts served one after another. By the 1800s, dessert was served as a one plate course. Today's dessert dishes are between 7¼ and 8½ inches across (Von Drachenfels 2000).

Bread-and-Butter Plate

This plate is used so that your roast beef gravy does not slide into your nice warm crescent roll. This plate measures 6 to 7 inches across. When the table is set, the butter spreader is placed directly on the bread-and-butter plate, either at the top of the plate or on the right side of this little plate. Its blade faces inward, toward the left.

If your host does not provide a bread-and-butter plate, be comfortable in placing your bread either on the left side of your dinner plate or on the tablecloth directly to the left of your dinner plate. The pat of butter will remain on your dinner plate. Use your dinner knife to spread the butter. Butter your roll on your dinner plate.

Tea Plate

This little plate is about 6 inches across and, of course, is used at tea. However, it can easily be interchanged with the bread-and-butter plate or used for serving an individual side dish. I have used this small plate beneath little dessert bowls of ice cream and under crystal glasses holding shrimp cocktails. When presented with a doily on top of it, the plate is called an *underliner.* An underliner with a doily is used to hold gravy boats, salad dressings, and other sauces that are passed around a table.

There are also small plates (about 7½ inches in diameter) that are made with a little well on the surface. These were designed so that a saucer is not required under the teacup. The teacup is placed directly on the plate (in the little well). Food is also placed on this same little plate. These are also called tea plates and are found at brunches and informal luncheons.

Service Plate or Charger

The service plate is between 11 and 14 inches across. It is laid on the table in the center of the cover before the diners are seated. Remember? The cover is the dining area in front of one diner. The service plate has several other names: cover plate, show plate, charger plate, buffet plate, lay plate, place plate, and liner plate. The term *service plate* is sometimes used to refer specifically to a small plate placed beneath a bowl or a cup.

The purpose of the charger plate is to hold the place for the diner's appetizer course or a predinner drink (also called a *preprandial* drink; this literally means "before a meal"). The rule of etiquette is that the guest should never experience an empty space in front of him or her unless awaiting the dessert course.

This plate is also used as a decorative piece at informal meals where its use is optional. Informally, the service plate may be colorful and made of china, wood, pewter, or other creative and casual materials. At more formal meals and in fine restaurants, this plate is meant to match the occasion and may be made of china or glass; it may be gold-banded or appear to be made of silver or gold.

The service plate is traditionally cleared after either the first or second course. If soup is being served, it makes good sense not to clear this plate from the table until the soup plate is cleared. The soup course could be the first course. Or, if the meal begins with a cold course, the soup would be the second course. Then, the charger would remain on the table for that second course.

Soup Bowl

Soup bowls come in a variety of shapes and sizes. The most common shape is the cereal bowl. It has no rim and is about 6 to 9 inches across. You have been acquainted with this bowl since you were four years old and your mother served you alphabet soup in it.

Soup Plate

Another instantly recognizable shape is that of the soup plate. The soup plate has a very shallow well, and its rim is exactly like that of a dinner plate. Its diameter is between 9 and 10 inches, but the well itself is where the soup sits. The well may be only 6 to 7 inches across. The good news is that you may tip the soup plate away from you, in order to eat any remaining soup, chicken, or vegetables that found their way to the bottom of your soup plate.

Bouillon Cup

A bouillon cup looks something like a teacup with two handles. It is served with a little matching service plate beneath it. The bouillon cup is used for serving a jellied soup or a hot broth. You may pick up the cup by either one or both handles to drink your soup. If the broth is served with a soup spoon, you have a choice. You may drink the soup by picking the cup up by the handles, or you may use your spoon to drink the soup. Decide which way you wish to drink your soup and stay with that method. Later in this chapter, in the section titled "How to Eat Soup," bouillon cups are again discussed.

Cream Soup Bowl

The cream soup bowl is very similar in appearance to a bouillon cup. It is a heavier cup and slightly larger. It is double-handled and is used for rich and heavy creamed and pureed soups. It is made in both small and larger sizes. You may choose to drink the soup by picking the cup up by the handles, or you may use your spoon to drink the soup. The cream soup bowl is discussed again in this chapter, in the section "How to Eat Soup."

CUPS

Cups are easy! There are only large cups and small cups. In the wonderful book *The Art of the Table*, author Suzanne von Drachenfels tells us that until somewhere in the 1600s, Europeans used tall vessels for their liquids and drank their beverages cold. With the advent of more trade routes, people were suddenly drinking coffee, tea, and hot chocolate. At that point, tall tankards, which had been used for cold liquids, just didn't work very well. Since these imported beverages were expensive, the first cups for warm beverages were very small. They were made of various kinds of stoneware and earthenware (Von Drachenfels 2000).

In 1708, hard-paste porcelain was created by two Polish alchemists, Count Ehrenfried Walter von Tschirnhaus and Johann Friedrich Böttger. They had actually been trying to magically turn everyday items into gold and silver. Augustus the Strong, King of Poland, had no plans to allow the formula for porcelain out of his country, so only deaf and mute workers were hired at the porcelain factory. Tight security or not, within fifty years porcelain was being made in Denmark, France, Holland, Italy, and England (Von Drachenfels 2000). In the mid-1750s, the Meissen porcelain factory began to produce teacups that had handles so that delicate ladies would not burn their fingers when taking tea.

The large cups are the breakfast cup, coffee cup, mug, and teacup. These may hold anything from steaming coffee in the kitchen and guacamole (and chips) in the den to flash drives and pencils in the office. Large cups can hold up to 16 ounces of liquid or several dozen pencils.

Small cups include the demitasse cup, small after dinner coffee cup or teacup, bouillon cup, and chocolate cup. Small cups can hold about 4 ounces of liquid (Von Drachenfels 2000). I grow little plants in antique teacups.

SERVEWARE AND HOLLOWARE

Serveware are the pieces, such as platters and trays, on which you serve a meal. Platters can be as small as 8 or 9 inches across and as large as 24 inches or more. At the holidays, you probably use a large platter on which to serve your turkey, roast, or ham. You might use a smaller tray to serve hors d'oeuvres or even cookies.

Bowls are also serveware. You would serve a big bowl of pasta, family style, at your dining table. Cake stands are serveware. Other types of serveware include nut bowls, candy dishes, and soup tureens. A soup tureen is a deep bowl that holds soup. In formal settings, the server places the tureen on a serving tray table and serves diners directly from this tray table.

Holloware is a type of serveware. Holloware is exactly what it sounds like: serving pieces that are hollow—like a teapot, gravy boat, or a lemonade pitcher.

GLASSWARE AND STEMWARE

Glassware is any nonstemmed drinking vessel. Glassware is used to serve cool beverages, such as water, iced tea, and lemonade. Glass *stemware* is glassware that has a stem. The stem sits on a flat foot. Wine, Champagne, and sparkling wines, all cool beverages, are served in stemmed glassware. Sorbet and ice cream may also be served in a stemmed glass. The only exception to serving cool beverages in stemmed glassware is the brandy snifter, which is used to cradle warm brandy.

In a traditional setting, five glasses are set to the right side of the dinner plate. They are set in the order of the service of the food they will accompany, all close to the top of the plate. The first is set to the diner's right and the others follow to the left of the first glass: aperitif glass, water goblet, white wine glass, red wine glass, and Champagne flute.

Be aware that crystal stemware is very thin and must be handled carefully. A Champagne flute may be made of crystal, and therefore any clinking that accompanies toasting must be done gently if at all. If you are at a diplomatic or white tie function, look around and see if others are clinking glasses before you clink.

Aperitif or Sherry Glass

At a very formal dinner, you will have an *aperitif* glass that is set closest to the plate. You pronounce this *"ahpaireeTEEF."* It is also called a Sherry glass and is held by the host or hostess when making a welcoming toast. It is only served at a table when it accompanies the first course, which is a soup (most properly, it is served when the soup also contains Sherry as an ingredient).

Water Goblet

This glass stays on the table throughout the meal and is never removed; it is refilled. It is the largest glass at the setting. The water goblet sits toward the top right of the dinner plate.

White Wine Glass

Its bowl is a little smaller than that of a red wine glass because this wine does not need as much room to "breathe." Breathing allows the aroma of the wine to be released, and connoisseurs say that it is better to concentrate the white wine's fine bouquet in this smaller glass. Most often, white wine is served with a fish or an appetizer course. Wine traditions do evolve, and it would not be improper, in an informal setting, for you to order a glass of white or red wine with your dinner, whatever the main course. Remember to hold the white wine glass by the stem. This wine is served chilled, and you do not want to warm the bowl.

Red Wine Glass

The bowl of this glass is large in order to allow the robust aroma of a red wine to be released, or to breathe. It is a little taller than the white wine glass. Reds are often poured with the entrée (main) or meat course, although today you will see fine reds being served with fish. You may hold this glass by its bowl or its stem since traditionally reds are served at room temperature.

A variation of the generic red wine glass with the large bowl is the Bordeaux glass. Bordeaux wine is any wine produced in the Bordeaux region of France, such as a Cabernet Sauvignon or a Merlot. This glass also has a large bowl, but the top of the glass is wider and turns outward to allow more air to reach the wine, allowing the wine to breathe. The wine's complex taste will be softened as it is exposed to the air.

This glass directs wine to the back of the mouth. A Burgundy glass has an even larger bowl so that the aromas of delicate reds can be directed to the tip of the tongue. Burgundy wine is any wine produced in the Burgundy region of France, such as a Pinot Noir.

Stemless Wineglass

Many trendy and casual restaurants and bars are using nontraditional stemless red and white wine glasses. A stemless wineglass resembles a short water glass that has a rounded bottom.

Champagne Glass

Three common Champagne glass shapes are the flute, tulip, and coupe. Experts say that glasses shaped like a *V* concentrate the bouquet of the drink. A more traditional shape is the coupe Champagne glass. It looks much like the glass serving piece in which you would receive sorbet. Champagne glasses, while remaining true to the traditional elongated shape, may also be stemless.

To be called Champagne, this wine must originate from the Champagne region of France. Otherwise, it's a sparkling wine. Champagne is properly poured with the dessert course. It is used for toasting at the end of a meal. It is also served as a cocktail. Hold this glass by the stem, as both Champagne and sparkling wine are served chilled.

Iced-tea (Iced-beverage) Glass

The iced-tea glass is both tall and narrow in order to hold lots of ice. This shape is perfect for serving cold beverages of any kind. Tomato juice, lemonade, and iced coffee are also enjoyed in the iced-tea glass. If your host has not provided a saucer beneath the iced-beverage glass, you must leave the spoon in the glass when you are through stirring your beverage.

HOW TO EAT

Different kinds of dishes have different etiquette rules. Knowing ahead of time how to deal with them will save you from making a mistake with an unfamiliar food.

How to Eat Salad

Your salad may be served with both a knife and fork or with a fork only. If served only with a fork, your salad has been either torn or chopped into controllable pieces. Eat your salad either Continental or American Style, using the same dining style with which you plan to eat the rest of your meal.

Unless you are assisting a small child, never cut up an entire salad. The broad salad leaves are first cut into manageable sections.

Then cut these sections into smaller pieces as you eat them, one bite at a time.

Use either the American or Continental style for your rest position. If you are using only a fork for your salad, when resting, the fork is placed in the 10:20 position, tines up. If you did not use the knife that was set for the salad course, then at the end of the meal, place it on the salad plate in the 10:20 position along with your salad fork.

Using either the American or Continental style, place your silverware properly when you are finished with your meal. This will assist your server in knowing that you are ready to have your plate removed.

Remember that in the American style of dining, you will be served salad before the main course. Continental style dining has the salad served after the main course and is the norm in Europe. You may also see Continental service at very formal meals in North America.

How to Eat a Seafood Cocktail

A seafood fork (also called a cocktail fork) will be served with shrimp, crabmeat, and lobster cocktails. The shrimp may be served in a stemmed glass with a saucer beneath it. If your shrimp have their tails on, you may pick each shrimp up with your fingers. Dip the shrimp into your cocktail sauce and then bite it off up to the tail. Place the tails on the saucer upon which the stemmed cocktail dish sits. Large shrimp are eaten in two bites. Shrimp served without the tails are eaten with the seafood fork.

Both crabmeat and lobster cocktails are also eaten with a seafood fork. If your seafood cocktail is served in a stemmed glass, please do not leave your seafood fork in the glass. Between bites, and when you are finished, place your fork in back of the stemmed glass on the saucer on which the stemmed glass is presented.

How to Eat a Fruit Cocktail

Fruit cocktail is eaten with a spoon. Your fruit cocktail will usually be served in a small dish or in a stemmed glass. Never leave your spoon in the dish or glass between bites or when you are finished. Place the spoon in back of the fruit cocktail's stemmed glass, on the saucer that is served beneath the cocktail, or in the 10:20 position if served in a dish.

How to Eat Soup

Eating soup in public can be a little challenging. Hold your soup spoon exactly as you would hold a pencil, as if you are writing. Make sure your thumb is turned up, not down. As with all dining implements, left-handed persons may reverse this position.

Spoon the soup away from you toward the center of your soup plate or bowl. Never blow on your soup; it will cool off soon enough. Never slouch into your soup or lean forward to meet the spoon. Bring the spoon to you. Do I have to mention no slurping?

Creamed and clear soups or broths are sipped from the side of the spoon. Soups that contain pieces of meat and vegetables, any hearty soup, and, of course, chili, are sipped from the front (the tip) of the spoon. Don't worry too much about your form. At a truly upscale dinner, you will not be served a hearty (read that as "messy") soup. Never order a hearty soup at a job interview meal.

A soup plate is a rather shallow bowl that has a rim, exactly like the rim of a dinner plate. If your soup is served in a soup plate, by all means grasp the rim with your left thumb and forefinger and tip the plate away from you to get every drop of the soup with your spoon. Tip with your right hand if you are left-handed. Never tip a soup bowl. A soup bowl looks like a cereal bowl.

If you are eating from a soup plate, when you are between sips or finished, you may leave the soup spoon in the bowl, in the 10:20 position. If a soup bowl or cup has a plate beneath it, leave the spoon on this serving plate between sips and when you are finished. Place the spoon in the 10:20 position at the back of the serving plate.

You will never properly leave your spoon in a soup bowl or cup. The exception is when you are dining very casually. Your bowl may have no plate beneath it. Then, you have no choice but to leave the spoon in the bowl in the 10:20 position, but never on the table or tablecloth.

As discussed earlier, a bouillon cup looks something like a teacup with two handles. It is served with a little matching service plate beneath it. It is used for serving a jellied soup or a hot broth. You may pick up the cup by either one or both handles to drink your soup. Or, if the broth is served with a soup spoon, you may wish to drink it entirely with the spoon. Choose one way or the other. Never use both methods during this soup course. Bouillon cups are traditionally used only at luncheons, but today they can be found at other informal meals, as broth works well with a lighter menu.

A cream soup bowl is very similar in appearance to a bouillon cup. It is a heavier cup and slightly larger. It is double-handled and used for rich and heavy creamed and pureed soups. It is made in both small and larger sizes. You will see this bowl of rich heavy soup served as a first course where the rest of the meal is lighter. The occasion may be a dinner or luncheon that is either formal or informal. You may choose to drink the soup by picking the cup up by the handles, or you may use your spoon to drink the soup.

At very upscale affairs, the server will ladle the soup into your soup plate directly from a tureen—a deep, wide, covered bowl. Tureens are quite heavy. The server places the tureen on a serving tray table and serves diners from this tray table. A tureen is an example of holloware. Smaller tureens are used to hold gravy, sauce, or vegetables. All tureens should have a matching service plate beneath them.

How to Pass, Butter, and Eat Bread

Take a moment before going directly for what you think is your bread plate. Your bread plate is the one that is just to the left of your dinner plate. Remember "BMW?" Your **B**read plate is on your left, your **M**eal is in the middle, and your **W**ater is on your right.

As the person closest to the basket of rolls, offer the basket first to the person on your left by saying, "Would you like a roll?" After he or she selects a roll, take one for yourself and then offer the basket to the person on your right, saying, "Would you like a roll?" After this person takes a roll or a breadstick, say, "Would you please pass the basket to the right?" If the table is small, only four to six people, then it would be proper to wait and take your roll when the basket comes back to you.

Take only one roll. You want to be sure that everyone at the table gets a roll or other piece of bread. The basket will come back around to you. Take a second roll later. If you are hosting a dinner and the tables are large, have more than one basket of bread or rolls on each table.

There is no such thing as a butter knife. Please do not call a butter spreader a butter knife. If there is a master butter plate, then this too is passed to your right. Use the master butter spreader to collect a pat of butter and place that pat on your bread plate. Then put the master spreader back on the master butter plate. Its blade faces toward the inside of the bread plate, not outward toward the other diners. Your own butter spreader remains on your personal bread plate. When you have finished using your butter spreader, place it in the 10:20 position on your bread plate (face the blade toward the inside of the bread plate, not outward toward other diners).

At some events, your roll or bread may be preset on your bread plate. A pat of butter may be there as well. At informal events and in casual restaurants, the butter may be wrapped in foil. Remove the foil and place it on the side of the bread plate.

To eat your bread or roll, break off one small piece of bread at a time. Butter only this one piece. You will break off, butter, and eat only one piece of bread at a time. Do all of this on the bread plate—it is not an exercise that should be conducted in midair.

A hot muffin should be sliced in half and both halves should be buttered while the muffin is hot. Break off one piece of the muffin at a time to eat. An English muffin should also be sliced in half and buttered. Pick up and eat one half of the English muffin at a time. Toast is buttered and then cut in half. Pastry may be cut in half or quartered before eating.

How to Eat Sorbet—The Intermezzo Course

Sorbet is the French word and *sherbet* is the English word for an ice made from the syrup of fruit. It may properly be served at any point during the meal, but most often it is served either prior to or just after the heaviest course, the main course. It is often served just after the fish course, to clear the palate.

Clearing the palate means that you've made sure there are no lingering flavors still in your mouth from other foods. Clearing the palate makes it easier to appreciate the new tastes of the next course. Sorbet is eaten with a spoon. Spoon this syrupy dessert away from you as you eat.

In the world of music, the word *intermezzo* means a composition that fits nicely between either two acts of a play or between two larger pieces of music. The sorbet course is referred to as the *intermezzo*.

Food historians tell us that the first time sorbet is mentioned in history, it involved the Roman Emperor Nero (54 to 68 AD). He had runners bring snow down from the mountains. The snow was mixed with honey and wine. An Italian noblewoman, Caterina de' Medici, who married Henry II, brought *sorbetto* to France in 1522. From there its popularity rapidly spread throughout Europe, where it was mixed with juice and fruit pulp (Arnot 2003).

During the 1600s and 1700s, not even the wealthiest of households had enough silverware to go around, so the sorbet course was used in Europe as a stalling tactic. While the guests ate sorbet, the servants had time to wash used cutlery to serve with the next course.

How to Eat the Main Course

In the United States and in English speaking Canada, the main course is called the *entrée*. Be aware that in Europe and Australia, *entrée* refers to a smaller course that precedes the main course.

Use your dinner fork and dinner knife to eat the main course. Never season your food before tasting it. Doing so may insult your host.

As with the salad course, cut only one piece of your meat, chicken, or fish at a time. Eat that one piece and then cut another piece. This is the correct procedure for both the Continental and American styles of dining.

Decide on the style of dining (American or Continental) for your meal and remember that if one of your dining utensils is not used, you will still place it on your plate at the end of that course.

Use the correct placement of silverware on your dinner plate to let your server know when you have completed your main course. Never, ever push your plate away from you when you have finished eating. This action is very impolite.

How to Eat Fish

Fish is presented on a salad, dessert, or fish plate; any medium sized plate will work. Hold the fish fork in your left hand, the tines facing downward. Grasp the fish knife as if you were writing with a pencil. This is a lighter grip than you would use if you were dining on chicken or steak, as fish is much easier to manage.

Your knife is used first to cut and then to push the cut pieces toward your fork (Continental style). If your fish is very soft and you are absolutely certain that it is boneless, then by all means use only the fish fork. At the end of the course, even though the knife is unused, be sure to pick it up from the tablecloth and place it on your plate, next to the fork, in the 10:20 finished position. The blade of the knife will always face the fork.

Should you be served a whole fish, it will be presented with the head facing to the left. With your knife, make an *H* on the body. First cut the long horizontal center part of the *H* right across the fish and then cut the two legs of the *H*. Pry open the skin and eat the flesh of the fish, starting from the head and working your way down to the tail. Lift the skeleton off with your fish knife and flip the skeleton over to the top or side of your plate. Now eat the underside of the fish.

When you order a whole fish, you may ask the server to remove the head and tail in the kitchen. To remove the head of the fish yourself, use both your fish fork and knife to detach the head by cutting it off around the gills before attempting to debone. The tail is easily sliced and separated from the fish. Remember to ask your server for a little plate on which to place the head and tail. It is correct to ask the server to remove this small plate from the table once it has served its purpose.

How to Eat Difficult Foods

Your career and personal life may now, and certainly will eventually, call for you to dine both formally and informally with management, vendors, guests, family, people in your own community, and possibly even global visitors. Let's face it. Some foods are just plain difficult to eat.

What follows is a list of many of those foods and how to eat them. If you forget exactly what comes next when dining out, take a deep breath, and watch your host. Follow his or her lead.

- *Artichokes*: The leaves are removed one at a time with your fingers. Dip the soft end of the leaf in the sauce provided. Pull the leaf through your teeth to eat the edible part. Place the inedible part on the side of your plate. You may scrape the center part (called the thistle or heart) with your knife and fork. Cut the heart into manageable pieces and eat these with a fork.
- *Bacon*: Eat very crisp bacon with your fingers. Otherwise, bacon is eaten with a knife and fork.
- *Baked potatoes*: Make a small cut in the top of the baked potato (if this was not done in the kitchen) and lightly squeeze the potato open with one hand. Using your dinner fork, take butter from your bread plate. Place the butter in the potato. Eat the inside of the baked potato first, American style, using a fork. Eat the skin with a knife and a fork. You may wish to eat the inside of the potato Continental style, using both a knife and a fork.
- *Berries*: Eat berries with a spoon. If strawberries are large and served with the stem still on, you may hold them by the stem and eat them in one or two neat bites. Large strawberries are served with sugar for dipping.

- *Caviar*: Caviar comes from the *roe*, or eggs, of a fish called a sturgeon. Caviar is served in a small crystal bowl that is set on a surface of well cracked ice. To the side of the caviar are either small round pieces of toast or little Russian pancakes (*blinis*). Spoon a small amount of caviar onto your toast or *blini* and add a drop of sour cream, chopped egg, and/or capers onto the caviar. This gourmet treat is eaten with the fingers.

- *Corn on the cob*: Save this vegetable for casual meals. Butter and season several sections at a time. Never butter the entire ear; that's just plain sloppy. Grasp the ear of corn securely in your hands and eat the sections you have buttered and seasoned. Butter and season the next section.

- *French fries*: French fries are cut in half and eaten with a fork. The exception to this rule is when the fries are served with a sandwich. Then they become finger food. French fries are also finger food at fast-food emporiums and drive-throughs (also called drive-thrus). French fries served with open-faced sandwiches are eaten with a knife and fork.

- *Fried chicken and other birds*: All birds may be eaten with a knife and fork. Small game birds may be taken apart with a knife and fork and eaten with the fingers of one hand. Fried chicken is generally eaten in public with a knife and fork. Fried chicken is properly eaten with the fingers at picnics, fast-food establishments, and in the family kitchen.

- *Frogs' legs*: Frogs' legs are held and eaten with the fingers of one hand. The legs are first disjointed with a fork and knife. Frogs' legs taste very much like chicken. The meat is white and tender.

- *Garnishes*: A garnish is a vegetable, fruit, or flower that is used to decorate the dinner plate. If these are edible, they may be eaten with a fork. Do not pick up garnishes with your fingers.

- *Lobster*: Separate the larger parts of the lobster with your hands. Pull off the claws. Crack the claws with a nutcracker.

Extract the tender meat with a cocktail fork. Or ask your server to have the lobster separated and cracked in the kitchen. Lobster is traditionally dipped in either melted butter or cocktail sauce. Never order a lobster at a business meal if you are the guest or if you are being interviewed. It is both a messy and inappropriately expensive choice.

- *Nuts*: Casually, nuts are eaten with the fingers. There may be no spoon in a dish of nuts. If there is a spoon, use the spoon to pick up the nuts and place them directly from the spoon onto your cocktail plate or cocktail napkin.

- *Olives, radishes, and other relishes*: Olives, radishes, pickles, baby carrots, and celery are eaten with your fingers. These finger foods are called relishes. If there is no serving fork, you may take the relishes from their tray with your fingers. At a meal, place them directly on your dinner plate. As cocktail party food, place them on a paper napkin or on a cocktail plate.

- *Oysters, clams, and mussels*: Use a cocktail (or oyster) fork for oysters, small steamed clams on the half shell, and mussels. Using your cocktail fork, dip these delicacies in the sauce or butter provided. Eat in one bite. If served on toothpicks, eat from the toothpick. Mussels served on the half shell may be picked up with your fingers and sucked directly from the shell. Large raw clams on the half shell are eaten with a seafood fork or the fingers. The rubbery neck sheath that cannot be eaten may be pulled off with the fingers. Dip and eat this large raw clam with your fingers. Place discarded shells in a separate bowl and dip the clams in broth or melted butter. When you have finished eating the clams, you may drink the broth using a spoon (or directly from the bowl). Fried clams are eaten with a fork.

- *Sandwiches:* Open-faced sandwiches are cut and eaten with both a knife and a fork. French fries served with open-faced sandwiches are eaten with a knife and fork. Eat small tea type sandwiches with your fingers. Cut club sandwiches with a fork and knife into quarter portions and pick up these smaller portions with your hands. The traditional sandwich that Mom made and is found on any casual restaurant menu is eaten with your hands.

- *Sauces*: Sauces are either poured directly onto or just next to the meat, fish, or chicken on your dinner plate. Never drown your meal with sauce.

- *Soft-shell and hard-shell crabs:* Soft-shell crabs are cut with both a knife and fork and eaten with the fork. The entire soft-shell crab is eaten—legs, shells, everything! Hard-shell crabs require that you pull away the larger pieces by hand and then pull off the claws. Eat only the meat in the claws of the hard-shell crab. You may need a nutcracker to crack the claws. Extract the tender meat from the claws with a cocktail fork.

- *Spaghetti*: This is a form of pasta. Pasta is a doughy noodle made in a variety of shapes. Spaghetti is long and thin. Pick up two or three strands with your fork and place the prongs of the fork against the side of your plate. Twirl the strands against the side of your plate until they are gathered onto your fork. Suck them quietly into your mouth. Do not use a spoon. Northern Italians will frown on the peasant-like technique of using a spoon for assistance. Most pastas are eaten with a fork. Ravioli is eaten with a spoon. Never order spaghetti or other pastas at an interview meal.

- *Snails*: With one hand, hold the snail shell with the tongs provided. With your other hand, use the oyster or cocktail fork provided to pull out and eat the snail. If there are no tongs, use your fingers to secure the shell. Using your other hand, pull out and eat the snail with the oyster or cocktail fork provided. If bread is served, it may properly be dipped into the garlic butter in which the snails sit.

- *Watermelon*: At a casual event like a picnic or barbeque, watermelon is eaten holding a cool, crisp slice in your hands. Otherwise, eat sliced watermelon with a fork. If it is served already cubed, eat it with a spoon. You will have to drop the seeds from your mouth directly into your hand and then place the seeds onto your plate.

How to Eat Dessert

Your dessert may be served with both a fork and a spoon. If this is the case, place the fork in your left hand (tines down) and use the fork to anchor the dessert. Use the spoon to eat the dessert. Baked Alaska, a gooey tart, or ice cream served on top of a brownie are desserts deserving of both a fork and a spoon.

Pie and cake are generally served and eaten with a fork only. A dessert like ice cream, pudding, or sorbet is served only with a spoon. If your dessert is presented in a stemmed glass, never leave the spoon in the glass. Place it in the 10:20 position at the back of the saucer on which the stemmed glass sits.

When you are finished, leave all utensils in the 10:20 position. Place the tines of the fork down and the bowl of the spoon up. If there is a piece of cutlery that you did not use, pick it up from the table and place it in the 10:20 position on your plate. If you are served dessert with only a fork, leave the tines pointing up and the fork in the 10:20 position after your meal.

If a plate of cookies or other sweets is passed around the table, take only one piece to make sure that there is enough for everyone at the table.

How to Drink Coffee or Tea

Coffee or tea may be served at your table during or after the dessert course. Sometimes coffee is served after the dessert course along with chocolate candies. Sugar and cream will be on the table. These are passed together. As the person closest to the sugar and cream, offer them to the guest seated to your left, serve yourself, and then offer them to the person seated to your right, saying, "Please pass these to the right."

Try not to make noise with your spoon when lightly stirring your coffee or tea. Leave the teaspoon at the back of your saucer, in the 10:20, finished position. Never place your used teaspoon back on the table. Even if you have not used your teaspoon, place it on your saucer when you have finished your coffee or tea.

Demitasse is a strong coffee traditionally served black and often without sugar. If you are served demitasse, you may request sugar if it has not been served with sugar.

If you are served a tea bag with your cup of hot water, remove the bag's wrapper and place the tea bag in the cup of hot water. Never place your used tea bag on your saucer. Ask your server for a small plate on which to place the used tea bag, or leave the tea bag in your cup.

Do not shake your packets of sweetener against the table before pouring the sweetener into your cup, and don't drain your tea bag by twisting it around your teaspoon; these behaviors not only lack elegance, but they also may make you look irritated and lacking in patience. Never pick up your tea bag by its string and dip it up and down. Again, it will appear that you lack patience. Fold your tea-bag wrapper and place it just under your teacup's saucer.

If you are given a pot of hot water, place the unwrapped tea bag in the pot; the tea bag will remain in the pot. Fold your tea-bag wrapper and either place it just next to the little dish that holds your small teapot or directly under this little dish.

In business, all of this can be very distracting, and you may appear untidy and disorganized. If you are dining with clients or guests, or if this meal is actually a job interview, I recommend that you simply order a cup of coffee.

In casual settings, with everyone at your table ordering coffee or tea, you will accumulate a variety of little plastic creamer cups, torn sugar packets, tea-bag wrappers, and used tea bags. Ask your server for a saucer on which to place these used items. If there is no saucer for your used packets of sweetener or sugar, fold the small packet and slide it just under the saucer on which your coffee cup or teacup sits. Do not move your coffee cup or teacup around the table once you have hidden your used sweetener packet.

I have a secret to avoiding all of this messiness. When ordering tea, I say to my server, "Will you please place the tea bag into the pot of hot water before the tea is brought out? Thank you." Problem solved.

How to Use a Finger Bowl

People ate with their fingers well into the mid-18th and 19th centuries. Fingerbowls were used in England and France as early as the 1800s. Today, you will see finger bowls at formal events in North America and, of course, in Europe.

Finger bowls are presented in one of two ways. In the most formal method, you are presented with the finger bowl just before the dessert course. It will be placed in the center of your place setting on an underliner. An underliner is a small plate or saucer with a doily resting on it. A fork and spoon will be resting on the underliner.

First, you must place the fork on the tablecloth, to the left of the saucer, and then place the spoon on the tablecloth, to the right of the saucer. Pick up the finger bowl and the doily with both hands, and set these at the upper left of your place setting. Leave the small saucer in front of you. Your server will then place the dessert course on the saucer.

In some circumstances, the finger bowl may be placed to the upper left of your place setting by the server. When dessert is finished and your server has removed your dessert plate, pick up the finger bowl and doily with both hands. Place these items directly in front of you. A less formal (and more common) use of the fingerbowl is when the bowl is simply placed directly in front of the diner when the dessert plate has been removed and the meal is at its end.

Dip one set of fingertips (only the fingertips, not the fingers) in the water at a time. After you dip the first set (your right fingertips), dry that set on your napkin, under the table, before dipping the second set (your left fingertips). Dry your second set of fingertips on your napkin, under the table. For informal dining, and in first class cabins of certain airlines, small, hot, damp towels may be presented to the diner by the host, restaurant, hotel, or cabin attendant just before the meal.

How to Properly Serve

Food is properly served from the diner's left side, and plates are removed from the diner's right side. Water and other liquids are poured from the right. Coffee and tea are served from the diner's right. So as not to hit your guest with your right elbow, serve all foods with your left hand. Place your fingers beneath the plate to support it. Your thumb will rest on the rim of the plate. Whenever practical, the server stands to the left of the guest when taking the order. Individual plates are never cleared until each guest at the table has finished that course. Then the next course is served.

You may experience a variety of styles of table service used in restaurants worldwide, including the following:

- *Plated service* is also called *American service*. It is the most informal service and is fast and efficient. The food is plated in the kitchen and served directly to the diner. This is the most common type of service found in restaurants and at large dinner parties.
- *English service* is also called *service à l'anglaise* (in the English manner). A server presents the food to the left of the diner, on a platter. The server then serves the diner directly from the platter, using a serving fork and spoon. English service is generally used for banquets because portions can be controlled based on the number of guests expected.
- *French service* is also called *service à la française* (in the French manner). Each guest is presented on his or her left with an arranged platter. A serving spoon (bowl up) on the right and a serving fork (tines down) on the left are on the platter. The guest serves himself or herself, taking the fork in the left hand (to keep the food steady) and the spoon in the right hand, bowl up (to lift the food). The guest will place the serving fork and spoon back in their original positions on the serving platter as a courtesy to the next guest.
- *Russian Service* is also called *service à la russe* (in the Russian manner). The servers present decorated whole fish,

meat, poultry, or game to the guests with great flourish on a platter. In view of the guests, the meal is then carved up on a side table that has a burner. Individual plates are then served. While generally rare today, this very high end service is found in some ultrafine restaurants around the world. It originated in the early 19th century.

How to Use a Napkin

The Spartans used to wipe their hands on sliced bread. The Romans used their cloth napkins for wrapping food to take home after a feast. When examining Dieric Bout's version of *The Last Supper* in Saint Peter's Church in Belgium, you will see a communal napkin on the table. We lost napkins altogether in the Middle Ages. Wiping the hands with clothing and bread seemed fairly convenient at the time.

Eventually, the French gave us the forerunner of today's napkin. The old French word *naperon* means "little tablecloth." It was a long towel that was laid over the couch on which an honored guest was to sit during the meal. A long towel was also placed in front of the master's place (Von Drachenfels 2000).

Today, in North America, the napkin is placed to the left of the cover. In Europe, you may see the napkin placed to the right of the spoon.

When you sit down at a dinner table, it is important that you do not touch anything on the table. This means that you do not reach for your napkin or for a piece of bread. Think of dining as a well orchestrated play. Everyone has to do what the script calls for.

If you are at a hosted diner, the host will pick up his or her napkin. This is your signal that the meal has begun. This is the proper method of placing your napkin in your lap:

1. Pick up your napkin.
2. With your left hand, pick up your napkin by its upper left corner. This is the corner opposite the fold. The fold is the right side of the napkin; the fold faces the plate.

3. With your right hand, grasp the lower right corner of the napkin.

4. Now just lift the napkin off the table and turn it right onto your lap.

5. Open the napkin so that the fold faces your waist. Never unfold the napkin all the way. The open part of the napkin is facing your knees.

In fine restaurants, be sure to wait before placing your napkin in your lap, as your server may also be trying to place your napkin in your lap. If the napkin is folded in a fancy manner or resembles either a swan or an erector set, simply place the entire creation onto your lap and unfold this art project under the table.

Worried about your napkin leaving small white specks of fuzz all over your black Armani slacks? Most upscale restaurants are able to provide you with a black napkin on request.

If you need to leave the table during the meal, your napkin is placed on the chair seat. Say "Please excuse me" to the persons seated on either side of you. There is no need for further explanation. Exit your chair from its right and push the chair under the table. When you return, pull the chair out and pick up your napkin. After seating yourself (from the chair's right), place the napkin back on your lap. In some establishments, staff may refold your napkin and place it either on the arm of your chair or to the left of your cover.

If you drop your napkin from the table, do not attempt to retrieve it. Politely ask your server for a replacement.

When your host picks up his or her napkin and places it to the left of his or her place setting, this is your signal that the meal is over. When you are ready to leave the table, pick up your napkin by its center and loosely fold it over. Place it to the left of where your fork was originally set. Exit your chair from its right side and push the chair under the table.

How to Use a Napkin Ring

The napkin, inside the napkin ring, is set on the table with its point facing the diner. Hold the napkin in your right hand. Pull the ring away from the napkin with your left hand. Place the napkin ring at the top and to the left of your plate and dining utensils. Place the napkin in your lap. Unfold the napkin under the table. The fold of the napkin is placed at your waist.

Your server will probably remove the napkin ring from the table. If not, at the end of the meal, loosely refold your napkin, pull it back through the ring, and place your soiled napkin to the left side of your dinner plate so that the point of the napkin faces the center of the table.

Originally, napkin rings were personalized so that each member of the family could easily identify and reuse his or her cloth napkin. This was before we all had washers and dryers. After World War II, napkin rings lost favor as paper napkins became popular for family meals. Today, napkin rings are used as a festive and decorative touch and are not used in formal dining.

WINE ETIQUETTE

I can't think of anything more nerve racking than being called upon to select and order wine for clients and guests. You'll need to please everyone. Not to worry! Here are the basics. If more than one wine is to be served during a dining experience, just remember to order white before red, light before dark, dry before sweet, and simple before complex. Each type of pouring requires a fresh wine glass. On second thought, just follow the advice below.

Selecting Wine with Some Help

Both sommeliers (knowledgeable wine professionals) and servers are there to assist you in choosing a wine. The sommelier will pair foods with the complementary flavors, aromas, and textures found in specific wines.

Ordering Wine on Your Own

If no sommelier is available, ask your server for assistance in choosing one wine that will work with the variety of entrées ordered by the table. This may not be possible if there are a number of very different entrées. Your options are to order two bottles or two or more splits of wine. One standard bottle of wine holds about four to six glasses. Ordering a split is like ordering a half bottle of wine. A half bottle pours two to three glasses.

Most restaurants have a nice house white wine and red wine. Order one of each of these wines for the table. If some guests are drinking and others are not, suggest that each guest orders what he or she wishes by the glass.

When in doubt, California Cabernets are a classic choice. If you are dining with sophisticated clients or guests, you will need to consult your sommelier well in advance, and you may need to consider a French wine. Or find out who the wine lover is in your group. Let this person make the choice. Say, "Bob, I'm going to bow to your superior knowledge as a collector of fine wines." Just remember that Bob does not know your price restraints.

How Much Should I Spend?

When the sommelier gives you the wine list, you can communicate your price range by pointing to a wine in that range. Say "Something in this area is good." Or "Something like this." He or she will understand your meaning.

Presentation of the Wine Bottle

Your server or the sommelier will present your selection with the label facing you as the host of the group. You will look at the label and nod as you are just verifying that this is the wine and the vintage you ordered. The vintage is the year that the grapes were harvested.

Inspection of the Cork

After uncorking the wine, the server will place the cork on the table. Feel the cork in between your thumb and first finger. It should be moist on one end. It should never be all wet or all dry. Nod to the server. You will not ever need to say anything at this point unless the cork is dry and brittle or completely wet. These conditions mean that your bottle was not stored properly. *Never sniff the cork.*

Tasting the Wine

Since you are the host, you will be offered a small sample of the wine. Swirl your glass a bit to release the bouquet of the wine. Rest your glass on the table as you swirl. Raise your glass and sniff the wine, then taste it to make sure that the wine has not spoiled. Is there a pleasant, lingering aftertaste? This is called the *finish*.

Not liking your selection is never a reason to send back the wine. The wine is only sent back if it is "off." An "off" wine is one that has a very moldy, musty, or vinegar-like scent and taste. When the wine has been overexposed to air, the taste of the wine is altered unpleasantly and the wine becomes "off."

I've Approved It. Now What?

After you've approved the wine, the server will pour for your guests. Ladies are served first, and the host's or hostess's glass is poured last. The various types of wineglasses are discussed in the "Glassware and Stemware" section of this book.

Corkage Manners

Often, guests wish to bring to a restaurant a wine that they enjoy and that is their own. This is particularly true in certain parts of North America. Restaurants generally charge a *corkage fee* for uncorking and serving your private bottle. The corkage fee covers both the service and some of the revenue lost from not selling you the wine. Please remember that the gratuity for serving you this wine is not added to the corkage fee.

Before bringing your own wine to a restaurant, telephone the restaurant to make sure that this practice is allowed. Ask what the corkage fee is. If the fee is very high, it may not be reasonable for you to bring in your own wine. Corkage fees in North America can range anywhere from fifteen dollars to fifty dollars per bottle. If this is a restaurant where you are well known or which you frequent often, the fee may be waived. If you are also ordering wine during your meal, the corkage fee for the bottle you brought with you may be waived.

Ask if your wine is on the menu. If it is, even if the vintage is different, it would be considered poor manners to bring to the restaurant a wine that is already served there.

Types of Wines

This is a book on business etiquette, not a book on wines. Nevertheless, you are hospitality professionals, and I want you armed with essential knowledge of the basic types of wine and related terminology. You'll hear the word *varietal*. A wine varietal is the type of grape from which the wine is made. A varietal must be made of at least 51 to 75 percent of that grape. By California law, wine varietals must have at least 75 percent of the grape. As an example, a bottle labeled "California Chardonnay" must contain at least 75 percent Chardonnay grapes. Excellent wines come from different countries: France, Germany, the United States, Chile, Italy, Portugal, Spain, Australia, New Zealand, South Africa, and many others. The following are the types of wines you'll need to know about:

- *Red wines* are great with meat, fowl, and cheese. In the red wine group, you will find Chianti, Barolo, Bordeaux, Burgundy, and Riolja (Rioja). Other red varietals include Pinot Noir, Cabernet Savignon, Merlot, and the Zinfandels. If it's called a Syrah, the grape was grown in either France or North America. The same red wine produced in Australia and South Africa is called a Shiraz. Rich reds are served between 59°F and 68°F (Baldrige 2003). Lighter reds are served between 54°F and 57°F (The Wine-Storage Cave 2013).
- *Rosé* is a lighter red wine made from red grapes whose skins have been removed. Serve this pretty pink-colored wine well chilled in hot weather.

- *White wines* go well with lighter foods like chicken, fish, shellfish, veal, fruit, salad, and other vegetarian offerings. Serve white wines chilled. The white wine group includes Chablis, Chardonnay, Sauvignon Blanc, Chenin Blanc, White Burgundy, ChasagneMontrachet, Meursault, Muscadet, Sancerre, Gavi, Pinot Grigio, and Rieslings (Baldrige 2003). White wine is best kept in the refrigerator, at about 46°F to 57°F, until served (The Wine-Storage Cave 2013).

- *Appetizer wines*: Appetizer wines are pre-meal drinks. An *aperitif* is an alcoholic drink meant to stimulate the appetite before a meal. *Apéritif* is pronounced "ahpaireeTEEF." There is no single alcoholic drink that can be called an *apéritif*. Champagne and white wine are examples of *aperitifs* as are Campari, Dubonnet and Sweet Vermouth. The last three are generally served with ice in a small glass. *Aperitifs* are usually served with salty peanuts or almonds.

- *Dessert wines* are drinks served after a meal. They may be poured either directly from the bottle or from a decanter. Sherry, Port, and Madeira are wines that are called *digestifs* (alcohol to help digest the meal) and are served at room temperature. Sweet dessert wines like Sauternes are served chilled. Serve Sherry and Port in small aperitif or Sherry glasses. Chilled dessert wines are served in white wine glasses (Baldrige 2003). The perfect service temperature for dessert wines is 43°F to 47°F (The Wine-Storage Cave, 2013).

- *Champagne and sparkling wines* are both served chilled. As discussed earlier in this chapter, to be called Champagne, this wine must come from the Champagne region of France. Otherwise, it's a sparkling wine. Asti Spumante is a sparkling Rosé from California. Champagne is properly poured with the dessert course and is used for toasting at the end of a meal. It is also served as a cocktail. Serve Champagne and sparkling wines at temperatures of between 43°F to 47°F (The Wine-Storage Cave 2013).

TOASTING ETIQUETTE

Toasting began in Greece. The host would drink to the guests' health and taste the wine to make sure that it was not poisoned. Early Christians clinked glasses to ward off the evil spirits that they believed entered the body through alcohol. The word *toast* comes from the Latin *tostum* and means "parched, scorched, or burned." Some say that this explains the word's association with drinking. People were parched, so they drank. I believe the term *toast* comes from medieval England. The English would traditionally add a piece of toasted bread to a jug of wine to reduce its acidity.

Toasting has evolved into a wonderful way to warmly greet your guests and clients, present your congratulations to colleagues, and wish a newly married couple a blissful life together. There are three customary toasts.

The Welcome Toast

The welcome toast is made by the host before eating. Your host will stand and simply say, "It's a pleasure to see all of you here today at the Third Annual Children's Hospital Awards Luncheon. Bon appétit." If there is only one small table of participants, then it is not necessary for the host to rise. Never clink your glass with a piece of cutlery in an attempt to get your audience's attention.

Toast to the Guest of Honor

The second toast is given to the guest of honor. It is offered during the dessert course and is traditionally made with Champagne. The host will rise and say something like, "We are here today to honor Mr. Alphonso Bookbinder. Mr. Bookbinder has worked tirelessly on behalf of the new Children's Hospital Oncology Wing. His efforts have ensured over 2 million dollars in community donations. Please join me in toasting Mr. Alphonso Bookbinder." The host will raise his or her glass, as will all attendees. Everyone drinks except Mr. Bookbinder. The person being honored does not pick up his or her glass. One never drinks to oneself.

Actually, even if you're not Mr. Bookbinder, you don't *have* to drink the Champagne. Say nothing when it is served to you during the dessert course. Simply raise your glass when the toast is made, or raise your water glass and sip your water. Since you are polite, you will choose not to draw attention to yourself.

Toast Given by the Guest of Honor

The third toast is given by the person being honored. Mr. Bookbinder rises and says, "I'm humbled by your compliments. This was a real team effort, and I worked with the best volunteers in the world. Please join me in thanking our host, Mr. John Joyful, for this wonderful luncheon." Everyone drinks except for the host, Mr. Joyful. Toasts are meant to be upbeat, but most of all, toasts are meant to be short!

TEA ETIQUETTE AND HISTORY

Afternoon tea is served anywhere between the hours of two and five o'clock. This means that business can be conducted in the late afternoon or early in the evening, and then everyone goes home. Traditionalists will tell you a proper tea starts promptly at three o'clock and ends at five, but that the hours of service can be altered a little.

In North America, business people are increasingly inviting associates and clients to afternoon tea. Many hotels specialize in afternoon tea. This is a light repast. Please don't call it high tea, thinking this means that the occasion is fancy. High tea originally meant a late and rather substantial sit-down meal for the working class in Great Britain. Everyone ate a big meal after returning home from the shops, factories, mines, and farms. Originally, high tea was called *meat tea*.

Some food historians will tell you that the term *high tea* comes from the expression "It's high time we eat." Others say that the word *high* refers to a time that is numerically high in the day. Still others say the term *high* refers to the high wooden tables that were used in pubs, or to the dining tables that were high and were set with a heavy meal. Today, this repast is served at about six o'clock in the evening. *Low tea* refers to a less substantial meal served on a tea table, usually a low coffee table placed in front of a sofa.

In addition to afternoon and high tea, there are four other types of tea service. *Cream tea* is a snack served with tea, scones, jam, and clotted cream. *Light tea* is a service that includes tea, sweets, and scones. A *full tea* is a four course meal consisting of tea, finger sandwiches, scones, sweets, and dessert. *Royal tea* is, again, a four course meal. It is served with the guest's choice of either Champagne or Sherry.

Ancient lore has it that tea was accidentally discovered during the 28th century BC by the Chinese Emperor Shen Nung. This emperor, known as a great healer, had observed that healthy people drank boiled water. One day when he was boiling water, tea leaves floated from a nearby bush into his pot, and a new drink was born that soon defined a culture.

Tea appeared in Paris in 1636, twenty-two years before it made its first appearance in England. Historians find five o'clock tea mentioned by a Madame de Sévigné in a 17th century letter she wrote to a friend. Madame de Sévigné was a prominent social journalist who wrote about King Louis XVI and his queen, Marie Antoinette, and other aristocrats. It was the French who added milk to tea, and of course, the English adored and copied this fancy French affectation (Burns 2014). Tea was a casualty of the French revolution because it was expensive and associated with the well-hated aristocracy. So the British became the keepers of all things tea.

Afternoon tea is historically credited to the beautiful Anna Marie, the seventh duchess of Bedford, a lady-in-waiting to Queen Victoria. In the 1840s, when there was no such thing as lunch, the duchess would have tea in the afternoon along with bread, butter, jam, and cake. Afternoon tea would tide her over until dinner. Soon, her friends were joining her, and a national and treasured tradition was born.

All teas come from the same source, the *Camilla sinensis* tea bush. There are four basic types of tea. Their flavors vary based not only on climate and soil, but also on the methods used to process the leaf. All of the various teas you see on the grocery store shelves are types of black, oolong, green, or white tea. The following are the differences among them:

1. *Black* tea is "withered" and allowed to ferment. English breakfast is a type of black tea.
2. *Oolong* tea is semifermented. Formosa is a type of oolong tea.
3. *Green* tea is panfired. Gunpower is a type of green tea.
4. *White* tea is steamed. The buds of white tea are plucked. China white is a type of white tea.

There are also flavored teas that can be any of the basic teas blended with natural flavors, such as orange or peppermint.

Herbal tea is not a tea at all. It is a crushed blend of herbs and contains no caffeine. The correct term for an herbal tea is a *tisane*, from a 14th century Greek word meaning "to crush." Tisane is pronounced "*teeSAHN.*" A *rooibos* is an herb grown only on the western coast of South Africa. It means "red bush" in Afrikaans and is pronounced "*ROYboss.*" It, too, is a caffeine free herbal tea.

*Yerba mat*é (pronounced "*YERba MAHtay*") is an evergreen member of the holly family. The Guarani Indians of Paraguay and Argentina introduced this herb to the world in the 1800s as a drink having medicinal powers. Today you can purchase this caffeine free herbal tea in many flavors.

At a proper tea, your host, hostess, or the person designated to pour will ask you if you want strong or weak tea. You will also be asked if you would like milk, sugar, or lemon. Let the person pouring know how you prefer your tea. If you want nothing added to your tea, you will say, "Plain, thank you."

At a traditional tea, the person serving will hold a sterling silver tea strainer directly over your teacup when pouring. Tea strainers catch stray tea leaves that may fall from the teapot into your cup.

Afternoon tea is a wonderful way to entertain guests or clients. Teas are given to welcome someone into the community or to celebrate a special occasion, such as a birthday or a professional achievement. Afternoon teas are often given during the holiday season.

The Food at Tea

The food at tea is served in courses. The first course (usually the bottom tier on a three-tiered stand) consists of tea sandwiches (also called savories) or similar finger food. The second course, served on the middle tier, consists of scones and sometimes pound cake. Scones (pronounced "*sconnz*") are small, sweet biscuits. They are the most popular food served at a tea. Desserts, such as pastries, cakes, tarts, and other sweets, are the third course. This course is served on the tray's top tier.

At a tea, it is appropriate to dine according to course, from the savory items to the sweet items. The legendary Four Seasons Hotel in Toronto, which has a very beautiful Tea Lobby and the most wonderful associates in the world, sets up its tea service in the traditional way that I have described to you.

You may, on occasion, find that the tiered stand has been set so that the scones are the first course (bottom tier) and the savories the second. This is how tea is served at the Fairmont Empress in Victoria, British Columbia. The hotel's Afternoon Tea Lobby is world famous; they have been setting up their charming tiered trays this way for almost one hundred years.

I have also seen tiered trays set with the scones placed on the top level. I will not debate which setup is correct and which service is not. I will say only that the savvy guest at tea will dine according to course, no matter where the courses are placed. Start with the savories.

Should you be taking tea in a private home, all three courses may be laid out on trays. You may place some of each of the three courses on your plate. You will not have to serve yourself three different times. You may return for more tea and food as many times as you wish, so there is no need to heap large amounts of food on to your tea plate. Depending on the formality of the event and the number of tea plates owned by your host, you may or may not end up keeping the same plate throughout the tea.

How to Eat Scones

To eat a scone, first spoon jam, butter, or cream onto your plate. Take a scone and slice it horizontally. Spread first the jam and then the cream on the bottom half of the scone. You may pick up this half and eat it one bite at a time. Or you may spread only one bite at a time on this half of the scone. Another option is to slice the scone in half and break off small pieces; put the spread on each piece before you convey the piece to your mouth with your fingers.

Some prefer to eat scones using a knife and fork. Slice the scone horizontally and spread first the jam and then the cream onto the scone's bottom half. The top half is eaten after you have finished eating the bottom half. Enjoy your scone using a knife and fork either American or Continental style. Never put the slices back together. Never eat the slices as a sandwich.

Teatime Tips

I know how uncomfortable it can be the first time you take tea in a formal setting. Teatime is meant to be enjoyable and relaxing. The only way to enjoy and relax is to know the rules. While the rituals of tea may seem daunting, I suggest that when taking tea, you follow the lead of your host. Enjoy this relaxing tradition for business or just for fun. Keep the following Teatime Tips in mind:

What to Do at Tea

- *Always* greet your host as soon as you enter your social or business tea.
- *Always* pour milk into your teacup *after* the tea has been poured into the cup.
- *Always* put sugar into your tea before adding lemon. Lemon prevents the sugar from dissolving.
- *Always* place the slice of lemon into your teacup after your tea is poured (and after you have added sugar). Leave the lemon slice in your teacup.

- *Always* hold your teacup by its handle with the index finger through the handle and the thumb above it as support.
- *Always* hold the teacup's saucer just above your lap if seated.
- *Always* place the teacup and saucer on a side, cocktail, or other table (if one is provided) when you begin to eat. Hold your small plate of food in one hand. With the other hand, eat your savories.
- *Always*, if seated and ready to drink your tea, temporarily place your plate of food on your knees.
- *Always* raise both the teacup and saucer together if you have placed them on a table.
- *Always* place one or two savories or sweets on the side of your teacup saucer and eat these with your fingers in lieu of holding both a teacup and a plate.
- *Always* place the teaspoon in the saucer behind the cup, away from your body.
- *Always* place a paper napkin beneath your teacup if there is a small spill in your saucer.
- *Always*, when in a restaurant, request a clean saucer if your tea has spilled.
- *Always*, when in a restaurant, request a saucer for your used tea bag.
- *Always*, when in a restaurant, place the folded tea-bag wrapper beneath your saucer, or if there is a pot of hot water, next to or beneath its saucer.
- *Always* place your silverware properly during and at the end of tea.
- *Always* maintain napkin etiquette.
- *Always* walk up to your host and thank him or her at the end of the tea.
- *Always* send your host a written thank-you note.
- *Always* adhere to all the rules of dining etiquette when at a tea.

What Not to Do at Tea

- *Never* put milk into the cup before pouring the tea; you won't be able to judge the strength of the tea.
- *Never* put a lemon slice into the cup before the tea is poured.
- *Never* put both lemon and milk into your teacup.
- *Never* remove cloves from decorated lemon slices.
- *Never* use your spoon to press the lemon slice that is in your teacup.
- *Never* cradle your teacup in both hands.
- *Never* extend your pinkie finger while drinking tea.
- *Never* swirl your tea.
- *Never* lift only your teacup from a table without lifting the saucer as well.
- *Never* leave a teaspoon in the cup.
- *Never* coil the string of a tea bag around your spoon.
- *Never* place a tea bag on your saucer.
- *Never* shake the tea bag by its string in hopes of speeding up steeping.
- *Never* heap large amounts of food onto your tea plate.
- *Never* clank or make any unnecessary noise with your spoon (Johnson 2005c).

FREQUENTLY ASKED DINING QUESTIONS

Have you ever experienced a really scary moment at the table? That split second when you believed that one wrong choice would cause the Etiquette Police to show up and haul you away to the Manners Underworld, a place of relentless embarrassment and shame? Wow! That's awful!

Here's the thing. Dining is supposed to be fun, so lighten up. This is the perfect time to enjoy your clients, friends, and family. If you do forget some small point of etiquette, just slow down and watch what your host and others around you are doing. You may see yourself in some of the questions and answers listed below. They are the dining questions I have been asked most frequently. Read these, practice, relax, and enjoy your dining experience.

Q: When may I begin to talk business at a business meal?

A: The conversation is social until the main course arrives unless both parties have agreed beforehand that this is a working lunch. If the business matter is of some urgency, then after the meal orders have been placed, it is appropriate to move the conversation toward your business agenda.

Q: I've dropped my fork or spoon. What shall I do?

A: You may accidentally drop your knife, fork, or spoon from the table. Do not attempt to retrieve the cutlery. Politely ask your server for a replacement. If the item puts a server or other guest in harm's way, simply nudge the item back toward the table with your foot. This advice also applies to dropped napkins. Do not pick a dropped napkin up from the floor. Quietly ask your server for another.

Q: How do I remove food from my mouth?

A: The general rule is that food comes out of your mouth the way it went in. If you ate the item with a fork, it would be removed that way. If it is finger food, you would remove it with your fingers. Having said that, do what is simplest. Either remove the food with your fingers or by quickly depositing it on to your fork. Then place this bit of food onto your plate. Hide this small piece of food, pit, seed, or bone under a piece of parsley or other food. Do not discuss the removal with anyone at the table. Just do it quickly. Do not draw attention to yourself. Absolutely never tent your hands or hold your napkin over your mouth to disguise this operation.

Q: How do I handle a spill at the table?

A: How embarrassing! You've spilled your water or wine on yourself, a dining companion, or the tablecloth. Remain calm. If you've spilled on yourself, politely say "Excuse me" to the person on either side of you and take care of the spill in the restroom. After you have left the table, you may ask one of the servers for some club soda for the stain. If you've spilled on someone else, *do not touch this person*. Apologize and offer your napkin. Get a server to bring some club soda for your dining companion. Quietly insist on paying the dry cleaning bill. Do so calmly. You should not make a small embarrassment into a larger one. The same goes for spilling on the table itself. The server will take care of this.

If you have spilled something in a private home, the host or hostess is sure to jump up and take care of it. You must privately speak with your host and insist on having the tablecloth dry cleaned or replaced. Since most hosts would never accept your gesture, you must both call and write a note of apology to your host or hostess. Depending on the damage and the relationship, consider sending flowers with your note of apology to the hostess.

Q: How fast should I eat?

A: Pace yourself throughout the meal. You do not want to be the first guest finished. You also don't want to be the last. Everyone else will have to wait to enjoy the next course if you dawdle. Be observant. Eat slowly if most of your dining companions are lagging behind you. Eat more quickly if you have been absorbed in conversation and notice that your table companions are close to finished with their meals.

Q: Where do my hands go?

A: In the American style of dining, when your hands are not in use, you may place them on your lap. It is also correct to leave one hand on the table (at the wrist) between courses. In the Continental style, you absolutely must leave both hands, placed at the wrist, on the table. This custom came from medieval Europe. The host wanted to see both hands of his guests to make sure there were no hidden weapons.

Q: May I push my plate away from me?

A: Never push your plate away from you at the end of either a course or the meal itself. Never stack your plates in an attempt to assist the server. Do not push your coffee or teacup away.

Q: When are the plates removed?

A: The waitstaff properly removes the guests' plates after each course, and only when each and every guest at the table has finished that course. It is a breach of dining etiquette to begin serving a course to some when others at the table are not finished with the prior course. The last two or three people who are still eating will become very uncomfortable if everyone else's plate has been removed.

Q: What if I use the wrong piece of silverware?

A: If you need a knife or a fork for the next course because you have used the wrong piece of silverware for an earlier course, ask the server for a replacement. Ask politely; there is no need to explain.

If you have not used your knife or other pieces of cutlery during your meal, upon completion of that course, place any unused silverware on the plate *in the finished position.* Cutlery is never left on the table when a course is completed. This holds true for both the American and Continental styles of dining.

Q: How do I enter and exit a chair?

A: Yes, there is a correct way to do even this! At a table for ten, picture everyone trying to be seated at the same time. It would look like a carousel. Simply enter your chair from the chair's right and exit the same way, and remember to push the chair under the table each time you exit.

Since business is gender blind, a woman will never expect a man to seat her at a business occasion. Should a gentleman wish to pull the chair out for a lady, the lady will simply say thank you, whether the occasion is business or social.

Q: How do I excuse myself from the table?

A: Both socially and in business, when you need to temporarily leave the table, simply smile and say "Please excuse me" to the people on either side of you. Do not give an explanation. Do not invite others to join you. This is not a caravan; this is a solitary trip.

Q: May I apply lipstick at the table?

A: Never apply makeup at the table. Say "Please excuse me," and go to the ladies' room. Do not invite other women to join you. In business, this reflects badly on your professionalism. Any activity that you would normally conduct in your bathroom (getting food out of your teeth with a toothpick, blowing your nose, fixing your hair, checking your contact lenses) must be conducted in the restaurant's, hotel's, or host's bathroom. To make sure that you do not leave lipstick stains on your napkin or on the water glass, I suggest that women blot their lipstick prior to the meal.

Q: May I blow my nose at the table?

A. The napkin is to be used for blotting lips. Never use the napkin as a tissue. If you must blow your nose, excuse yourself and blow your nose in the bathroom.

If, in an emergency, you must sneeze at the table, turn away from your seatmates to do so. If you must use your napkin to cover the sneeze, say "Please excuse me" to those on either side of you. Rise and take your napkin with you. Find your server or other employee. Let this person know you have soiled the napkin because of a sneeze. Ask that the napkin be replaced. If this person is not your server, tell him or her where you are sitting. Finish your nose blowing and hand washing in the restroom.

Q: How do I properly drink from a glass?

A: When you take a drink, look downward into the glass. Never look at your tablemates over the rim of the glass. This will lessen your credibility. Take sips of water either between conversation or after you swallow your food.

Socially and in business, drinking water (or iced tea or a soda) is not meant to be an exercise in washing down large amounts of food. Think of how the soiled glass will look to your associates, clients, guests, or host.

Q: May I accept food from someone else's plate?

A: Never accept food from a friend's or client's plate. Simply say, "No thank you." Remember to smile. Never offer others a sample of food from your plate. Eating from someone else's plate is not correct social or business behavior. Your client may actually be offended should you make such an intimate and unhygienic offer.

Q: How do I correctly pass food?

A: When passing items for the first time, pass all items to the right. If an individual diner requests an item that is nearest to you, simply pass the item in the most efficient way possible. Even if the diner only requests one of them, salt and pepper are always passed together. Items with handles—such as a creamer, a syrup pitcher, or a gravy boat—are passed with the handle pointing toward the recipient.

As the person closest to the basket of rolls, offer the basket first to the person on your left by saying, "Would you like a roll?" After he or she selects a roll, take one for yourself and then offer the basket to the person on your right, saying, "Would you like a roll?" After your dining companion selects a roll or a breadstick, say, "Please pass the basket to the right." Earlier in this chapter, in the section titled "How to Pass, Butter, and Eat Bread," this subject is discussed in detail.

Q: What's the etiquette of seasoning food at the table?

A: Since you do not want to insult your host, taste your food before using any seasonings. This is especially true if the meal is held during a business meeting or an interview. Could you be making assumptions (about the seasoning) before you have all of the facts? Your interviewer or potential client may be observing your use of judgment.

Q: Where do I put used packets of sweetener?

A: When sweetener in packets is passed, take no more than two packets. You want to make sure there is enough sweetener for everyone at the table. After passing the sweetener container to your right, tear off a corner of your packet and empty the contents into your coffee or tea. Fold the small packet and slide it just under the saucer on which your coffee cup or iced-beverage glass sits. Do not shake your packets of sweetener against the table before pouring the sweetener into your cup. Do not move your coffee cup or iced-beverage glass around the table once you have hidden your used sweetener packet.

Q: I have restrictions on what I can eat. What should I do?

A: For special meal concerns (an allergy, religious, or vegetarian restriction), speak with your host prior to the event. If this is not possible, speak privately with the caterer, maître d', or restaurant manager either before the event or the moment you arrive. If the meal has been preselected, find a simple option. One option is a plain piece of fish. If you have shellfish allergies, or if you do not eat pork, ask for chicken. If you do not eat meat, ask for a vegetable plate. You can always fill up on bread and quietly order a baked potato and a salad. Try your best to arrange this well before the event.

Q: What are the guidelines for ordering alcohol?

A: During the social hour, you may have a cocktail, and at dinner functions, it is appropriate to order a glass of wine with dinner. In certain situations, such as a midday business meeting or a job interview, do not order alcohol. If you are hosting a business guest and your company does allow the purchase of alcohol during a business meal, you may ask your guest if he or she would like a cocktail or some wine.

If your host orders beer at a casual business function and you also want beer, ask the server for the brand you prefer or ask what they have on draft. Drink your beer from a glass, never from the can, unless you are watching a softball game at your company's annual picnic. Consume alcohol in moderation.

Q: How do I decline alcohol or other beverages?

A: If wine or other beverages are being poured at an event, never cover a glass with your hand. The server may end up pouring water or wine on you. Lightly place your fingertips on just the rim of the glass, smile at the server, and say, "No thank you." You may politely decline your host's offer of alcohol by saying, "Thank you, I think I'll have some iced tea this afternoon."

Never turn over a cup or a glass of any kind. Simply say, "No thank you." Never order a drink at a business meal if your host does not order a drink. Socially, your host may choose not to order a drink but insist that you do so. This is fine as long as you order one drink only.

Q: How do I handle cocktail party food?

A: Business cocktail receptions are about business. Hold your drink or food in your left hand. Your right hand must be clean, dry, and available for shaking hands. There is no gracious way to juggle cocktail party food.

The foods served at these events are called *hors d'oeuvres* or *canapés*. They are small snacks, such as cheese, meat, vegetables, or fish. They may be served on a cracker, a miniature piece of toast, or a little piece of bread. They may be eaten with fingers or a utensil. They may be served on a plate, or you may be given a paper cocktail napkin when you are served.

If this is a business event and there is a photographer wandering around taking pictures, you may not want to be snapped holding an alcoholic beverage.

Q: What's the etiquette for buffet lines?

A: Buffet service may be the choice of your host at your next business or social meal or reception. Buffets can be found in the most informal and most elegant of venues. The rules are straightforward. You must stand in line and wait your turn. Think of this as an opportunity to meet new people and to network. In some buffet lines, there may be servers who carve meat and game and serve these to you. Other buffet lines are strictly self service.

Use the serving forks, spoons, or tongs that are provided for you. If a serving utensil is missing, ask for one. Use a serving utensil only for its intended dish, and when you're done, return it either into the food or place it in the provided saucer or holder. See that the handle does not touch the food in the serving dish.

No fingers in the serving plates! No eating directly from the serving plates. No matter how tempting, do not start sampling your food while still in line. You are dining with others, so please don't touch food or put food on your plate and then place it back into a buffet serving dish. Never lean forward into the food to smell or sniff it, and of course, if you get food on your fingers from the serving pieces, absolutely do not lick your fingers. If you touch a piece of bread, you own it. Do not put it back because you've changed your mind.

If you must cough or sneeze, step away from the buffet line. If you have not sneezed into a handkerchief or a tissue, then as a courtesy to others, wash your hands before reentering the line. You are touching everyone else's serving pieces! Be mindful of your long sleeves, cuffs, sweaters, ponytails, and dangling jewelry. These items can inadvertently be dipped into the serving plates.

Please don't pile food onto your plate, making it impossible for your tablemates to see you! An overfilled and sloppy plate will look very unappetizing. Do not mix courses on one plate. No one wants to see the roast beef gravy running into the cheesecake on your plate. Take smaller portions and go back two or three times.

Leave your used plates and silverware on the table; a server will clear these for you. Return to the line and take a clean plate. If there is a beverage dispenser, be careful to ensure that the rim of your glass does not touch this equipment. Carry back to the table what can reasonably be carried. You only have two hands.

In buffet etiquette, the point is to eat while your food is still hot. You do not have to wait for the entire table to be seated. Do wait for two or more of your companions to join you. If you are taking a child through a buffet line, you may want to explain the rules about using serving utensils in lieu of fingers.

If this is a business occasion, remember that others are watching, and it's to your advantage to observe the basics of table manners.

Q: May I visit the table of someone I recognize?

A: This is called *table hopping.* When you see someone you recognize in a restaurant, smile and say hello as you pass his or her table when you enter or leave the restaurant. Do not stop at your colleague's table. After you are seated, you may smile and nod from your own table if you see someone you know. Never stop and stand over your acquaintance's table. In business, it would be rude to go over and expect that person to interrupt a business meal to stand and introduce you to his or her guests. Of course, you would want to very briefly visit the table of a relative or close friend.

Q: What should I know about dining at an interview?

A: The interview is not about food. The host is getting to know you and your qualifications. He or she also wants to see how you behave in public. As nice as he or she is, remember that this is a test of your social skills. He or she will greet you with a handshake. Shake your host's hand, maintain eye contact, and smile. Have a snack before you go to your interview meal so that you can concentrate more on the conversation than on the food.

Never order foods that are difficult to eat. Don't order spaghetti, open-faced sandwiches that have gravy on them, or anything that drips. Do not order either the least expensive or the most expensive item on the menu. Do not order alcohol even if you are invited to do so. Never take a doggy bag home with you even if your host suggests this. Send a thank-you note immediately after the interview.

Q: What if my host wishes to say grace?

A: Your obligation as a guest is to be respectful. If your host leads a prayer before a meal, your job is to sit respectfully with your head and eyes tilted down slightly. It is not necessary for you to say anything.

Q: What are my duties as the host?

A: Arrive early and be ready to receive your guest. After that, your most important duty as host is to see that your guest is comfortable. You may ask your client for his or her food preferences prior to making your reservation, but the choice of the restaurant itself is yours.

Choose a restaurant where you are known, or visit the restaurant prior to your business meal, introduce yourself to the maître d', and reserve a table that is not too close to the kitchen or to the entrance. Make sure that you have the privacy you need to conduct business. If time is of a concern, ask the restaurant to have the table preset with rolls, butter, and a pitcher of iced tea.

When your guest arrives, the maître d' will guide you to your table. He or she will walk first; the guest is next, and then the host. If there is no maître d' and you are guiding your guest, then you will walk in front of your guest, saying, "Let me show you to our table." When leaving the restaurant, your guest precedes you.

As the host of more than one guest, you will sit at the head of the table with your most important guest seated to your right. At a long table, the host sits in the middle. Regardless of who sits to the right, always seat your client in the most important seat. This is usually the chair that faces out into the room. You may seat yourself with your back facing the room.

An easy way to let your guest know your price range is to say something like, "The filet mignon is excellent, and you need to start with one of their amazing appetizers." Your guest will not know if it is appropriate to order wine or another alcoholic beverage unless you order an alcoholic beverage for yourself. Alcohol may be appropriate at a business dinner, but not at a business lunch. This may be spelled out for you by company policy.

All electronics are turned off at this meal. If you are awaiting an important call, let your client know that you may be excusing yourself during the meal for a matter that cannot wait. Place your telephone on vibrate. Do not place it or other electronics on the table. Do not answer your cell phone at the table. You may discreetly place your silenced cell phone out of sight, on your lap.

If an associate or a friend stops by your table, remember to stand up and shake his or her hand. Always rise. Always introduce this person to your client. After a little polite conversation, it's perfectly all right to say, "It was great to see you, Bill. Please excuse us; we have some business to finish up." Shake hands again and sit down.

If your guest checked a coat, as the host, you will pay the coatroom attendant's tip for both of your coats as you exit the restaurant.

Q: What if my best client insists on working with electronics at a business meal in a fine dining restaurant?

A: Electronics (cell phone, tablet, and other electronic items) of any kind are never placed on a dining table. As the host, this action puts you in the position of looking unschooled in manners. Suggest to your client that the two of you can comfortably work back at the office after the meal. If that is clearly impossible, and your client insists on working with a tablet, laptop, or other electronic device, then wait until after the meal is cleared. Remember, your most important duty as host is to see that your guest is at ease. Be as discrete and quiet as possible so as not to disturb other diners.

Q: What are my duties as the guest?

A: Be punctual. All electronics are turned off. Electronics are never placed on the table. Wait for your host to sit first before seating yourself. Your host may have designated a particular seat for you and other guests.

Ask your host what he or she recommends on the menu. This will give you an idea as to the appropriate price range. As a guest, you will never order either the least expensive or the most expensive item on the menu. Order something in the midprice range. The person who extended the invitation is the person who pays for the meal.

If an associate of your host stops by the table, he or she will be introduced. Always rise and shake hands.

Never ask for a doggie bag after an interview or business meal. You do not want to leave the impression that you cannot afford to pay for your next meal. If this is a business meal, consider carefully before ordering an alcoholic beverage. If your host insists that you order a drink, do so if you wish. Never order more than one drink at a business meal.

If you are dining informally at your host's private home, it is appropriate to bring a small hostess gift to the meal. Chocolates or gourmet cookies are both excellent choices. If you know that the couple or individual giving the dinner drinks wine, a bottle of good wine is always very nice. Do not expect your gift to be opened that evening.

Flowers, if not in a vase, present the host or hostess with the awkward situation of abandoning his or her other guests to search for a container. You may want to send flowers the next day along with a thank-you note if this was a special occasion. These suggestions are for small dinner parties only. Hostess gifts are not brought to large or formal parties, as your doing so may embarrass the other guests.

Q: What is the etiquette of paying the bill?

A: Whoever does the inviting pays for the meal. If you are the host, arrive early and give the maître d' or server your credit card. Depending on the number of guests and what is customary in your area, ask the maître d' to put the appropriate percentage gratuity on the card, and sign the charge slip before your guests arrive.

If you have not arrived early, then when you receive your menu, let the server know that you are hosting the meal and that you will be receiving the check. If you are hosting the meal on your property, let the server or maître d' know ahead of time that the meal and tip will be charged to the property.

FINAL DINING GUIDELINES

Readers always ask for easy dining guidelines. They want the opportunity to review table behavior before an event where their manners will be showcased and where their CEO may be watching. Below are two lists: dining reminders of what to do "always," and dining reminders of what "never" to do at the table.

What to Do at the Table

- *Always* set your electronic devices on "vibrate" or "off" during both social and business meals.
- *Always* let your guests know when you are expecting a telephone call and will need to excuse yourself during the meal.
- *Always* excuse yourself from your guests should your cell phone vibrate. Say, "Please excuse me."
- *Always* answer your cell phone or other electronic device in the hallway or outside, away from the dining table.
- *Always* remove your Bluetooth headset, or Glass, before entering a restaurant.
- *Always* chew with your mouth closed.
- *Always* keep your elbows off the table.
- *Always* say "Excuse me" if you accidentally burp, cough, or sneeze.
- *Always* place your left hand over your mouth if you cough. Your right hand must be germfree so you can confidently shake hands or pass food.
- *Always* cut only one piece of food at a time.
- *Always* wait until the meal is over and the dessert and coffee are served before placing memo pads and work folders on the table unless you and your guest have agreed to a working lunch.
- *Always* make polite conversation with the dining companions seated to your left and to your right.
- *Always* stay away from alcohol at a business meal. If your host insists, order only one drink.
- *Always* blot your lipstick before dining. You do not want your imprint appearing on either a glass or your host's cloth napkin.

- *Always* ask the server for a saucer on which to place your used tea bag, or leave the tea bag in your teacup.
- *Always* thank your host for the breakfast, lunch, or dinner at the close of the meal.
- *Always* write a thank-you note. Sending a thank-you note after a business meal will again put your name in front of your host. If your host is someone you know well, a thank-you telephone call or an e-mail is minimally the right thing to do.
- *Always* send a written thank-you note after a job interview meal. If the interview was for a technical position, then an electronic thank you is appropriate. If your host has corresponded only electronically with you in all matters, you may want to consider if a telephone call or an e-mail may, in this case, be the wiser thing to do.
- *Always* send a written thank-you note if the interview meal was for a job where you will have any kind of in-person, public contact.
- *Always* say please and thank you when speaking to your server.
- *Always* speak quietly to the maître d' about poor service if you are the host.
- *Always* quietly let the server know if your food is undercooked or has a foreign object in it. Do this only when dining out socially. Do not draw negative attention to yourself at a business meal.
- *Always* sit up straight. No one will notice your posture until you slouch.

What Not to Do at the Table
- *Never* place electronics (cell phone, tablet, and other electronic items) of any kind on a dining table. This puts you in the position of looking unschooled in manners.

- *Never* have your cell phone or other electronic ringer turned on during a meal. The person dining with you is the person who is important at that moment.
- *Never* place purses, briefcases, keys, sunglasses, or any object not related to dining on the dining table.
- *Never* speak with food in your mouth.
- *Never* form a tent with your hands to cover your mouth if you have filled it with too much food. This will draw attention to your error.
- *Never* order messy foods (like spaghetti or a sloppy joe sandwich) at a business meal.
- *Never* order ketchup in a high end restaurant.
- *Never* season your food before you have tasted it.
- *Never* take a sip of water when your mouth is full of food.
- *Never* ask for seconds until you have finished most of the food on your plate.
- *Never* wipe soiled utensils with your napkin. Politely ask the server for a replacement.
- *Never* pick up a dropped utensil or a napkin from the floor (unless you're at home).
- *Never* reach across someone else's plate to retrieve an item.
- *Never* eat from someone else's plate.
- *Never* chew ice in public.
- *Never* clink your glass with a piece of cutlery in an attempt to get your audience's attention.
- *Never* say anything about poor service if you are the guest.
- *Never* use a toothpick at the table or in public.
- *Never* push your plate away from you.
- *Never* think of lighting a cigar, cigarette, or pipe after a meal.
- *Never* blow your nose at the dining table. Do this in the restroom.
- *Never* apply makeup at the table.

CHAPTER 14

Global Etiquette
Multicultural Awareness

When Euro Disney opened its doors in France, alcohol was prohibited in the park. Disney failed to look carefully at a most historically important part of the national culture: French wine. Eventually, Disney corrected this blunder in order to show cultural respect and to do business in France.

The career that you have chosen makes you a citizen of the world. Each of your guests and fellow employees brings with him or her a cultural tapestry rich in history, customs, generosity, innovations, and expectations. You'll need to learn about other cultures and bridge your own cultural unknowns through multicultural competence if you are to successfully represent both yourself and your brand.

SENIORITY AND DEFERENCE

In North America, we tend to be relaxed and informal in most business interactions. This is not necessarily the way the world works. Issues of rank and seniority, if not handled properly, may derail your business plans. Do your research. If your global guest, client, or vendor is a high level executive, VIP, or other person of prominence, make sure this guest is received by an executive of equal rank. To do otherwise is an insult and shows a lack of respect.

Research your guest's culture so you can interact appropriately. Err on the side of formality at all times. Use proper titles, names, and complete addresses in all written contacts. Use high quality stationery. Silence can be an asset in international business. It's okay not to be speaking all of the time. Be professional, formal, and respectful in e-mails, texts, on the telephone, and in person. Practice proper introductions. Remember that your guest's name is said first in any introduction.

YOUR APPEARANCE SHOWS RESPECT

The first time your guest meets you, a lasting impression is made. It is critical that you maintain proper eye contact and excellent posture, and that you shake hands correctly. Research your guest's country before your meeting. Be certain that strong eye contact is appropriate in his or her culture. Your respectful business presentation includes an appropriate business suit for men and women alike. The fabric should be of the best quality that your budget allows. Your shoes should be clean and polished, and like your suit, they should be the best that you can afford.

Earlier in this book, I addressed the importance of wearing a good watch and carrying a quality leather portfolio or briefcase because your guest will be judging your appearance. Handbags must be made of an excellent quality of leather. A professional appearance is one way that you show respect for your visitor.

INTERNATIONAL BODY LANGUAGE, GESTURES, AND HANDSHAKING

Stance may send a positive or negative message. Greet your guest by standing with your shoulders facing his or her shoulders. Do not place your hands on your hips or cross your arms in front of your body. Never straighten your clothes or touch your face or hair. Remember to maintain good posture. Smile. Your hands will remain straight down, by your sides. This will convey a relaxed and competent appearance.

Even gestures have different meanings in different countries. No thumbs up, okay, or "V for victory" signs. These are highly inappropriate in several countries and may have vulgar meanings. Try not to gesture with your hands at all. Do not nod your head up and down, as depending on where you are, this may mean that you agree or disagree. Never touch your international (or any) guest unless it is to shake hands.

While you would never give a second thought to crossing your legs in North America, in many countries this sends a negative message of premature familiarity. Worse still is draping one foot over your knee, exposing the sole of your shoe. Middle and Far Eastern cultures find the bottoms of feet and the soles of shoes to be terribly offensive. Crossing your legs and showing your soles is certain to make you look disrespectful. I suggest that you keep both feet planted firmly on the ground while conducting business with guests from any country.

In Latin American countries, the woman initiates the handshake socially and in business. In Asian countries, women may only nod. In Germany, when a man is introduced to a woman, he must wait to see if she extends her hand. French women will initiate a handshake. The accepted French handshake is a light grip with one brisk stroke. If a man offers his hand to a woman in an Islamic country it is seen as highly offensive.

Generally, in North America and most European business settings, either a man or a woman may initiate the handshake. In social settings in North America and in Europe, a man may wait for a woman to offer her hand. Never pull your hand away from an international guest too soon, as this may indicate rejection.

Be aware of not only your body language but also of the personal space considerations of your client's country. Your guests from the Netherlands, Western Europe, Great Britain, and Asia will tend to stand rather far away from you. No matter how uncomfortable you are, do not move forward.

Latin Americans and citizens of Arab countries stand so very close that North Americans and many Europeans often find themselves stepping back to maintain a comfort level. Do not move back; this will be offensive to your international guest. Hold still and let your foreign guest set the ground rules.

Unsure of how to proceed? You may want to research the protocol of your guest's country. Or if you are on unfamiliar ground and do not want to create an international incident, see if your human resources department has access to the services of a certified international protocol consultant. This person can brief your team. Business customs differ dramatically from country to country. Be prepared!

In chapter 1, "Making a Five Star Impression," issues of personal space, positive body language, and gestures are discussed.

GUIDELINES FOR TOUCHING AND KISSING

Other than the handshake, avoid physical contact with your clients and guests unless you have studied the culture. The rules of touching vary from country to country. Some countries are touch friendly; examples are Italy, Greece, Spain, Russia, Latin American countries, and some Asian nations. Your Arab business counterpart may take your hand as you walk along. This is a sign of respect and friendship between two men. Do not pull away, as this would be a tremendous insult.

Your clients and guests from countries including Japan, the United States, Canada, England, and any Scandinavian country will not want to be touched by strangers. Pats on the back for a job well done will not be welcomed. Remember that in observant Arab and Israeli communities, men do not shake hands with women.

Never pat a child on the head. In Asian cultures, this is an action used only on dogs and would be an insult to the child's parents. While speaking and listening to your guest, foreign or domestic, remember to keep your hands at your sides and avoid any unnecessary gestures.

While Europeans may greet you with a kiss on both cheeks, Bulgarians and Russians will kiss you three times, going from cheek to cheek to cheek. You may have done your research but are still unsure of how to proceed. Hold still and take the appropriate cues from your guest or host or hostess. Remember that the senior person offers his or her hand first. Your guest is always the senior person. In business settings, be aware that age will often take precedence over youth.

INTERNATIONAL BUSINESS CARD PROTOCOL

In chapter 1, business cards were reviewed generally. There are some differences when discussing the use of business cards internationally. You may be conducting business in a country where your nation's language is not the primary language. If so, have a professional interpreter design a dual language business card for you. Your nation's language will be on one side and your host's language will be on the other side of the business card. Business cards are carried in a conservative card case. Remember to present your business card with the language of your host country facing the person receiving the card.

Research either the country you are about to visit or the country of your new guest. In Asian cultures, give your business card to the recipient with both hands; the card is presented with the printed side facing the recipient. Should your guest give you a business card, receive it with both hands. Take your time and read it in front of the guest. Do not write on your guest's business card. This shows disrespect. Never jam the card into a pants pocket. Place it in a purse, inside coat pocket, or in your portfolio to show respect.

HIGH- AND LOW-CONTEXT CULTURES

To communicate effectively with your global visitor, consider whether he or she is from a culture where people have close relationships for a long time or where relationships are traditionally of a shorter duration. These are called *high-context* and *low-context* cultures. In high-context cultures, everyone seems to be on the same page; in low-context cultures, behavior and beliefs may need to be spelled out so that everyone knows what is expected of him or her. Think about this when conducting business.

High-Context Cultures

In high-context cultures, information is less formal, and understanding may be based on long term relationships. There are insiders and outsiders. Families, clubs, and religious groups are good examples. Knowledge is situational, and decisions may be made centrally. Consider this when waiting impatiently for a business response. The relationship is more important than the business at hand (Hall 1959).

It can be very difficult to break into a high-context culture that is not your own. As an outsider, be patient and know that it takes time for social and business relationships to grow. High-context cultures include China, France, Japan, Spain, Arab countries, and Latin America.

Low-Context Cultures

In low-context cultures, communications are often written and more formal. Relationships are of a shorter duration. These cultures are task centered, and knowledge is more transferable. The task is what is important, not the relationship. A low-context culture would apply to behavior in a supermarket, cafeteria, business seminar, or game of soccer (Beer 2013).

Outsiders generally have an easy time conducting business and creating social relationships with members of low-context cultures. Low-context cultures include Canada, the United States, Switzerland, Germany, and Scandinavia. Do your cultural research so that you know how to behave and what to expect.

MONOCHRONIC AND POLYCHRONIC SOCIETIES

The way people view time and the way they behave based on time varies depending on their culture. Countries where people do one thing at a time, never miss a deadline, stick to plans, focus narrowly on the job, and expect short term relationships are called *monochronic* societies. Countries where people do many things at once, may or may not stick to time commitments, easily allow for interruptions, change their plans often, and build long term relationships are called *polychronic* societies.

When working with a guest from a monochronic society, expect agendas, schedules, and deadlines to be taken very seriously. Since it is harder to establish relationships with a monochronic culture, consider scheduling a greater number of shorter meetings so that rapport can be built. The United States, Canada, and Western Europe are all monochronic cultures.

Developing relationships is important to your guests from polychronic cultures. Spend more time with your guests to establish rapport and get to know individuals. You may want to consider polite conversation before diving right into business so that a comfort level is built. Latin American countries, the Mediterranean, Eastern Asia, China, and Arab countries are all polychronic societies. Use this knowledge when meeting new guests or establishing business relationships.

The Japanese maintain a polychronic society yet demonstrate great flexibility when dealing with Western cultures and are famous for using monochronic behavior during business encounters.

AVOIDING VERBAL AND WRITTEN CONFUSION

There are plenty of pitfalls when corresponding or speaking with international colleagues or customers that you might not anticipate. Here are some to keep in mind.

Day, Date, and Time

When speaking with your global guests and clients, consider that the world has different ways to communicate concepts of time (1800 hours versus 6:00 p.m.) and dates (August 23, '18, or 23,8,18, or 08/23/18, or 23-8-18, or August 23, 2018). Address time in a way that is easily understood by your global visitor. Consider this in both written and electronic communications.

Be considerate when telephoning, e-mailing, texting, or using Facebook, Skype, FaceTime, LinkedIn, or other devices and electronic media to contact your international friends and guests. Remember that the globe is divided into twenty-four time zones. Could your international client or guest be sleeping?

Measurements

The world also uses different measurements. There are liters versus gallons and meters versus yards. Consider this before addressing your international guest on matters related to measurements.

Abbreviations and Acronyms

Abbreviations and acronyms should not be used. An *abbreviation* is a shortened form of a word, such as "msg" instead of "message." An *acronym* is a word that is formed from the first letters of other words, such as CEO for chief executive officer. Play it safe. Using unfamiliar abbreviations and acronyms is inconsiderate because your guest may be embarrassed to tell you that he or she cannot understand what you've said.

Slang

Slang is the use of informal words and expressions that are not standard in the user's language. Never joke or use slang. Slang is sure to be misunderstood. When you use slang, you are implying that the listener understands what you are talking about. An example of slang would be to use the term *cab* instead of Cabernet Sauvignon.

Jargon

Jargon is the vocabulary of a particular profession. It may be appropriate to use jargon when speaking to a group people who are all members of the same field. Check with a knowledgeable professional before using jargon when speaking with your foreign guests. An example of restaurant jargon is using the term *seaboard* instead of saying that you want to take your dinner order home.

Idioms

Idioms are words or groups of words that, when translated from one language to another, fails to convey the correct meaning. Examples are *kick the bucket* (to die) and *knock your socks off* (to impress). Use terms that are clear and that everyone in your international audience will understand.

Humor

Humor is not easily translated electronically or in person. Be certain to leave a professional greeting on your voice mail. Do not make jokes. Do not take the chance of being misunderstood and insulting your guest.

INTERNATIONAL GIFT GIVING

Business and social gift giving protocols will vary based on the country of the recipient. A general rule is that the gift should not be too personal. Contemplating airport security inspections, do not prewrap your international gift. Either bring gift wrapping paper with you in your luggage or have your hotel's concierge take care of the wrapping. You must research the appropriate colors for wrapping paper. Even flowers have good and bad meanings depending on the culture.

Whether you are bringing a gift to a client in another country or planning to present a gift to an international visitor, remember that there are appropriate and inappropriate gifts. You would never present chocolates to the Swiss because the finest chocolates in the world are made by the Swiss. Generally, in Europe, you are safe presenting books, good liquor, gifts for children, and fine porcelain items. Never give flowers or anything terribly expensive.

Latin American clients will appreciate chocolates and gifts for the whole family. Stay away from flowers, wrapping paper, and gifts that are purple or black in Latin American countries, as these colors are associated with funerals. Never give a knife. This represents cutting the relationship.

Never appear at a client's home without a gift except in England and Ireland, where hostess gifts are not expected. South Korean guests will appreciate status items and good Scotch. Those from Arab countries are partial to gifts for their offices. Extravagant gifts are not appropriate in this culture.

Japanese guests enjoy North American brands; remember to present gifts to these guests with both hands. In both the People's Republic of China and Taiwan, it is common to host banquets for your client and the other members of his or her business team. To the Chinese, white represents death and mourning. Clocks are inappropriate gifts in Asian cultures (Johnson 2005a). Clocks can have bad *feng shui,* believed to be a specific energy that can weaken or strengthen the home. Just to be polite, Chinese guests may refuse your gift up to three times before accepting. Be ready for this possibility.

You must do your research to ensure both your guest's comfort and your own credibility. It is possible that your client or guest really must refuse your gift. His or her organization's policy may prohibit the acceptance of presents. Be gracious should this circumstance occur. Perhaps you can have the client and his or her team join you for a welcoming meal.

FLAG ETIQUETTE

You may be thinking, *Why has she included the topic of flag etiquette in a book about hospitality management and business behavior?* Flag etiquette is about respect. The highest standards of respect are the foundation of this grand industry. While federal law in most countries stipulates many aspects of flag etiquette, the general idea is that the flag of any nation is a symbol of inspiration and promise.

Your property displays your country's flag. You must always treat great symbols with reverence. The following is an outline of American flag etiquette that will serve as your guide when displaying the American and other flags on your property:

- The American flag and the flags of other countries are displayed between sunrise and sunset.
- The American flag, when flown after dark, must be illuminated.
- Fly the American flag only in fair weather unless yours was specifically designed for use in all types of weather.
- The American flag is displayed on the left side of a main entrance when viewed from a street or a sidewalk.
- When displayed with other flags (such as those of a state, county, city, citizens' organization, or corporation), the American flag is placed in the center and higher than the other flags.
- The American flag is raised and lowered before the flags of other countries.
- No international flag is flown higher than another in peacetime. When displayed with flags of other nations, the American flag is flown at the exact same height as all other national flags. The American flag is placed on the right (the audience's left), with the other flags to its left.
- When more than one flag is displayed from the same flagpole, the American flag must always fly on top.
- When displayed in an auditorium or other room where there is a speaker, the American flag is placed on the stage to the speaker's right (the audience's left). If there is a state or company flag onstage, it is placed to the left of the speaker, on the audience's right.
- If you are displaying the American flag with another flag and you are crossing the staffs, the American flag must be

on the right (the viewer's left). Its staff must be in front of the staff of the other flag.

- It is not appropriate to display more than one American flag at any event.
- When carried in a parade or procession, the American flag is held pointed to the flag's own right. If other flags are being carried in the procession, the American flag is carried directly in the center of the front of that line. The person carrying the American flag is called the *standard bearer*. The standard bearer leads the procession of flags.
- Americans salute the flag in a procession. If not in uniform, citizens place their right hands over their hearts. If you are wearing a hat, you should remove it and place it over your heart.
- The American flag is never dipped toward any person, not even the president of the United States.
- The American flag is not a decoration. Never drape a podium with the American flag.
- When displayed in a corridor, the flag is on the left side of the door as viewed by guests entering the office.
- When displayed in an office, the flag is set to the right of the seat that is behind the desk.
- During a meeting, the American flag is set behind and to the right of the person conducting the meeting.
- You will never fly your American flag at half-staff unless this has been ordered by the president of the United States or the governor of your state.
- On Memorial Day, the American flag (by order of the president of the United States) is displayed at half-staff from sunrise until noon. It is raised to full-staff at noon and lowered at sunset.
- Your flag and the flags of other nations where your brand has properties are symbols of pride. See that they are cleaned and mended as necessary.

CHAPTER 15

Saving the Best for Last
Creativity

The most creative and farsighted person I know of in this extraordinary business is Isadore Sharp. Mr. Sharp is the founder and chairman of the Four Seasons Hotels and Resorts. Now that, in and of itself, should be enough; but that's not why he's amazing. Mr. Sharp is the man whose creative visions redefined the industry's standards of service. How? Well, he's the first person who thought it would be nice if every guest had a little bottle of shampoo in his or her shower! Remarkable!

He used both common sense and uncommon savvy to effect an industry wide change. He also thought each guest needed a remote control for his or her television, a lighted writing desk, twenty-four hour room service, twenty-four hour secretarial services, twenty-four hour cleaning and pressing, a really substantial bathrobe, and let's not forget, an on property fitness facility!

You may be new to this remarkable industry. That doesn't mean you need to leave your creativity and individuality at the door. Things don't always have to be done the way they were always done. Maybe you can think of a way to do things better or with more joy.

Your creativity and resourcefulness make you an incredibly valuable asset to your team, to your brand, and to the guest experience. Speak up when you have a fantastic idea, even if it's as small as a tiny plastic bottle of shampoo. Creativity drives cultures of excellence.

LEADING WITH YOUR HEART

Christopher J. Nassetta is the president and chief executive officer of the Hilton Hotels Corporation. He was the keynote speaker in 2009 at the Third Annual National HR in Hospitality Conference and Exposition, held in Orlando, Florida. Mr. Nassetta spoke about corporate culture being "like DNA." He said, "But culture doesn't just happen. It's cultivated." And, "The right people don't think they have a job, they think they have a responsibility" (Nassetta 2009).

This industry leader's formula for success is more valuable than gold. Believe in and nurture your brand's culture. Be the person who cultivates an incredibly positive guest, team, and brand experience. Be the person who has a responsibility, not simply a job. Lead with both your talent and your heart.

I hope that you will refer to this book whenever you need a gentle push forward into the world of business and personal success.

Remember to send thank-you notes and keep your cell phone on vibrate. Remember your water glass is on the right and your bread plate is on the left. Assume that people will do what's right, and always listen with kindness. You are the best in the industry!

REFERENCES

American College of Neurology. 2000. "Often Missed Facial Displays Give Clues to True Emotion, Deceit." *ScienceDaily*, May 4. http://www.sciencedaily.com/releases/2000/05/000503181624.htm.

Arnot, Sharon. 2003. "Cool Off with Sorbet." *Sauce Magazine*, June 27. http://www.saucemagazine.com/a/895.

Bayne-Powell, Rosamond. 1972. "The Coaches." In *Travellers in Eighteenth-Century England*, online at http://www.ourcivilisation.com/smartboard/shop/bynpwllr/coaches2.htm.

Baldrige, Letitia. 2003. *New Manners for New Times*, 3rd ed., rev. New York: Scribner.

Belge, Kathy. 2011. "Coming Out at Work: Things to Consider Before Coming Out at Work." About.com Lesbian Life. Accessed October 13. http://http://lesbianlife.about.com/od/comingout/a/OutatWork.htm.

Beer, Jennifer E. 2013. "Communicating Across Cultures: High and Low Context." Culture at Work. Accessed July 23. http://www.culture-at-work.com/highlow.html.

Boothman, Nicholas. 2000. *How to Make People Like You in 90 Seconds or Less*. New York: Workman Publishing Company, Inc.

Borchers, Callum, 2014. "Google Glass Embraced at Beth Israel Deaconess."

Accessed April 9. http://www.bostonglobe.com/business/2014/04/08/beth-israel-use-google-glass-throughout-emergency-room/WhIXcVzkpn7MOCAhKuRJZL/story.html.

Bremer, Jill. 2004a. "Cubicle Etiquette." Jill Bremer Executive Coaching. http://jillbremer.com/articles/etiquette/cubicle-etiquette/.

_. 2004b. "Techno-Etiquette." Jill Bremer Executive Coaching. http://jillbremer.com/articles/etiquette/techno-etiquette/.

Brown, Robert E., and Dorothea Johnson. 2004. *The Power of Handshaking: For Peak Performance Worldwide*. Herndon, Virginia: Capitol Books, Inc.

Burns, Karen. 2014. "Tea and the Guillotine." *TeaMuse Monthly Newsletter*, September. http://www.teamuse.com/article_000902.html.

Cooper, Jeff. 2013. "The Origins and Early History of Tennis." About.com Tennis. Accessed November 10. http://tennis.about.com/od/history/a/earlyhistory.htm.

Eggers, Sandra. 2012. "Tennis Court Etiquette." BellaOnline. Accessed October 10. http://www.bellaonline.com/articles/art26699.asp.

Evenson, Renee. 2007. *Award Winning Customer Service: 101 Ways to Guarantee Great Performance*. New York: AMACOM.

Fox, Sue. 2001. *Business Etiquette for Dummies*. New York: Wiley Publishing, Inc.

George, Phillip. 2014. "Coin Clipping." History House. Accessed February 5. http://www.historyhouse.co.uk/articles/coin_clipping.html.

Gross, Kim Johnson, and Jeff Stone. 2002. *Dress Smart Men: Wardrobes That Win in the New Workplace*. New York: Time Warner Book Group.

Grotts, Lisa. 2009. "Yachting Etiquette." AML Group. Accessed February 20. http://www.amlgroup.com/etq-yacht.html.

Hall, Edward T. 1959. *The Silent Language*. Garden City, New York: Doubleday.

Ingram, Leah. 2005. *The Everything Etiquette Book: A Modern-Day Guide to Good Manners*, 2nd ed. Avon, MA: F+W Publications, Inc.

Johnson, Dorothea. 2005a. "How to Succeed in the International Arena." Speech presented at the meeting of the Protocol School of Washington, Portland, Maine, March 13.

_. 2005b. "Outclass the Competition." Speech presented at the meeting of the Protocol School of Washington, Portland, Maine, March 12.

_. 2005c. *Tea and Etiquette: Taking Tea for Business and Pleasure*, 2nd ed., rev. Sterling, Virginia: Capital Books, Inc.

Lavington, Camille. 2001. *You've Only Got Three Seconds: How to Make the Right Impression in Your Business and Social Life*. New York: Broadway Books.

Leboeuf, Michael. 2000. *How to Win Customers and Keep Them for Life*, rev. ed. New York: The Berkley Publishing Group.

Leutert, Werner. 2013. "For Professionals: Compensation." Home Staffing Network. Accessed January 4. http://www.homestaffingnetwork.com/professionals.php?id=3.

Maysonave, Sherry. 1999. *Casual Power: How to Power Up Your Nonverbal Communication and Dress Down for Success*. Austin: Bright Books.

Meyer, Danny. 2006. *Setting the Table: The Transforming Power of Hospitality in Business*. New York: HarperCollins Publishers.

Michael, Angie. 2000. *Best Impressions in Hospitality*. Albany, New York: Delmar Thompson Learning.

Michelli, Joseph A. 2008. *The New Gold Standard: 5 Leadership Principles for Creating a Legendary Customer Experience Courtesy of the Ritz-Carlton Hotel Company*. New York: McGraw-Hill.

Mitchell, Mary. 2004. *The Complete Idiot's Guide to Etiquette*, 3rd ed. New York: Alpha Books.

Nassetta, Chris J. 2009. "A CEO's Perspective on HR in the Hospitality Industry." Keynote speech presented at the 3rd Annual National HR in Hospitality Conference and Expo, Orlando, Florida, March 17.

Pachter, Barbara. 2008. "Eat, Drink and Be Smart: 9 Ways to Avoid Disaster at Your Office Holiday Party!" Rowan University PRSSA, November 17. http://ajfprssa.blogspot.com/2008_11_01_archive.html.

PokerSource. 2013. "Casino Tipping Etiquette." PokerSource.com. Accessed October 25. http://www.pokersource.com/poker-articles/casino-tipping.asp.

Post, Peggy. 2004. *Emily Post's Etiquette*, 17th ed., rev. New York: Harper Collins Publishers, Inc.

Reynolds, Donna. 2012. "Proper Business Meeting Etiquette and Manners." HowToDoThings.com. Accessed August 18. http://www.howtodothings.com/careers/a2494-how-to-practice-business-meeting-etiquette.html.

Sanders, Ed, Paul Paz, and Ron Wilkinson. 2002. *Service at Its Best: Waiter-Waitress Training, a Guide to Becoming a Successful Server*. Upper Saddle River, New Jersey: Pearson Education, Inc.

SIGA. 2013. "A Few Tips on Hospital Etiquette." SitaGita. Accessed November 28. http://www.sitagita.com/view.asp?id=8885.

Straker, David. 2006. "Mehrabian's Communication Study." ChangingMinds.org, January 1. http://www.changingminds. org/explanations/behaviors/body_language/mehrabian. htm.

Strunk, William, Jr., and E. B. White. 2000. *The Elements of Style*, 4th ed., rev. Needham Heights, Massachusetts: Longman.

The Memphis Center for Independent Living. 2014. "How to Interact with People Who Have Disabilities." AccessMaine. Accessed February 27. http://www.accessmaine.org/TipSheets/ InteractwithPWDTS.htm.

The Wine-Storage Cave. 2013. "Temperatures for Wines." Wine-Storage.com. Accessed July 18. http://www.wine-storage. com/info.html.

Tisch, Jonathan M. 2007. *Chocolates on the Pillow Aren't Enough: Reinventing the Customer Experience*. Hoboken: John Wiley & Sons, Inc.

Tour Canada. 1996. "A Brief History of Golf." http://www. tourcanada.com/golfhist.htm.

Tuckerman, Nancy, and Nancy Dunnan. 1995. *Amy Vanderbilt Complete Book of Etiquette: 50th Anniversary Edition*. New York: Doubleday.

US Department of Justice. 2013. "Information and Technical Assistance on the Americans with Disabilities Act." ADA. gov. Accessed January 3. http://www.ada.gov.

US Department of Labor. 2013. "Providing Quality Services to Customers with Disabilities." Office of Disability Employment Policy. Accessed January 9. http://www.dol. gov/odep/pubs/ek98/provide.html.

US Equal Employment Opportunity Commission. 1980. "Guidelines on Sex Discrimination." *Federal Register* 45, no. 219, November 10, 74676–74677.

Von Drachenfels, Suzanne. 2000. *The Art of the Table.* New York: Simon & Schuster.

Waldman, A. 2005. "Some Employees Wrestle About Coming Out of the Closet at Work." Gay News Blog, November 4. http://www.gay_blog.blogspot.com/2005/11/some-employees-wrestle-with-coming-out.html.

Wikipedia. 2012. "Aria." Accessed November 7. http://www.wikipedia.org/wiki/aria.

Wikipedia. 2013. "Medical Tourism: United States." Accessed January 7. http://en.wikipedia.org/wiki/Medical_tourism#United_States.

Wikipedia. 2014. "Google Glass." Accessed April 9. http://en.wikipedia.org/wiki/Google_Glass.

Zunk, Amy R. 2012. *How Rude! PDA and Cellphone Etiquette in the New Millennium.* Geek.com. Accessed November 18. www.pdageek/ features/cybermanners/index.html.

INDEX

Bluetooth/wireless earpieces/ MP3 players, etiquette, 30, 63, 143, 147, 223. *See also* electronic technology

body language
  international, 227–9
  positive, 12–13
  space, personal, 10–11, 228

bouquet, bride's, 38

boutonnière, 149

bowls. *See also* cups; cutlery; glassware/stemware; plates
  bouillon cup, 177
  cream soup, 177
  finger, 194
  serveware and holloware, 178
  soup, 176
  soup plate, 176

bus, travel by, 87, 104. *See also* business travel

business cards
  international, 230
  your brand, 14–15, 56, 80, 84, 126–7

business letters, 119. *See also* correspondence

business meal, 61, 63, 160, 190, 211, 216, 217, 219, 220, 221, 222, 223, 224, 225

business meeting, 30, 32, 61, 63, 64, 67, 142, 215, 216

business travel. *See also* clothes, dressing when out and about; clothes, how to dress on property
  packing wisely, 78–80
  travel essentials, 77–99
  types of transportation
    air, commercial, 80–2

bus, 87, 104
helicopter, 84
jet corporate, 82–3
limousine, 89, 96, 102, 104
rental car, 87–8, 101
ship, 84–5, 103
taxicab, 88–9, 95, 103
train, 61, 85–7, 103
yacht, 85

C

cake, cutting, 38

cameras, cell phone, 65. *See also* electronic technology; telephones, manners for

captain, 85, 87, 105, 106

career goals and ambitions, 27–8

Catholic traditions. *See also* Jewish traditions; Muslim traditions; Protestant traditions
  baptisms and christenings, 41
  confirmation, 44
  first communion, 43. *See also* Mass; Sacrament
  funeral, 53

celebrations. *See also* weddings
  baby showers, 40–1
  birthdays, 45, 46, 124, 207
  debutantes, 45–6
  family-related, 48
  graduation, 47
  holiday party, 47
  quince/quinceañera, 46
  sweet sixteen, 45
  work-related party, 48

celebrities, on property, 64–5, 138–9

G

H

Z

Lightning Source UK Ltd.
Milton Keynes UK
UKOW04f1833280415

250516UK00001B/96/P